# CROSSING AMERICA FOR A CURE
## A BICYCLE JOURNEY OF INSPIRATION AND HOPE

# CROSSING AMERICA FOR A CURE
## A BICYCLE JOURNEY OF INSPIRATION AND HOPE

## AL DECESARIS

**Al DeCesaris**
**www.aldecesaris.com**

Cover Image © 2013 by Grant L. Gursky

Cover Design © 2014 by Little Bit Heart

Book Layout © 2014 BookDesignTemplates.com

**Crossing America For A Cure: A Bicycle Journey Of Inspiration And Hope / Al DeCesaris** – 1st ed.

ISBN-13: 978-0692284308

ISBN-10: 0692284303

*To my beautiful niece Jenna*

*Thank you for opening my eyes and inspiring me*

**All profits from the sale of this book fund Sturge-Weber Syndrome research**

To help further the efforts to find a cure, purchase a copy of Al DeCesaris' latest book, *Running The Coast For A Cure: One Man's Journey For His Niece With Sturge-Weber Syndrome.* The book chronicles his extraordinary 1,935-mile East Coast charity run to create awareness and raise funds for Sturge-Weber research.

We exist temporarily through what we take, but we live forever through what we give.

Douglas M. Lawson

# Foreword

Inside us all lies an immeasurable force, the ability of ordinary people to do extraordinary things. What separates those who tap into that force is truly unknown, but people are driven for different reasons. Having known Al DeCesaris since we were 14-years-old, I can truly say I had never seen him ride a bike and, to be honest, wasn't even sure he knew how. But this is not about how to ride a bike or how far he could go, it is about that immeasurable force.

Every journey must start with the first step or, in this case, the first crank of the pedal. Each pedal stroke more tiring than the former but more important as it led him that much closer to his ultimate goal. This goal was not about personal recognition or accolades for an amazing accomplishment only a handful of people have achieved. Al biked across America for his niece Jenna, who was born with a rare neurological disorder called Sturge-Weber Syndrome. He did it to create awareness and raise funds for the research and treatment of the disorder.

Although he rode alone for the majority of his journey, Al was never really alone. From the Pacific Ocean to the Atlantic, he carried with him the thoughts and the prayers of family and friends. More important, he carried with him the hopes of those afflicted with Sturge-Weber Syndrome and their families.

I am certain you will read this story and be inspired by Al's journey. However, the true inspiration and beauty of his journey was not in traversing our amazing and breathtaking country, but in the people he met along the way, the lives he touched and those who touched him. That immeasurable force has resulted in an amazing journey for a great cause, inspired by Jenna and all of the children with Sturge-Weber Syndrome, and driven by the hope for a cure.

Bryan D. Springer, M.D.
Charlotte, NC

# Preface

On June 13, 2004, my sister Ida Heck gave birth to a beautiful baby girl named Jenna. Yet, what should have been a joyous occasion for Ida and her husband Ed was overshadowed by fear and uncertainty, for the right side of Jenna's face (from her hairline to the lower part of her cheek) was covered with a pronounced reddish-purple discoloration, and her right eye was abnormally enlarged. Although the obstetrician said it was just bruising from childbirth, Ida soon learned that it wasn't a bruise at all, but rather a permanent nevus on the skin known as a port-wine birthmark. A few days later, my sister was informed that her newborn also had glaucoma in her right eye and might even be suffering from something far worse.

Although it took over six months to determine, an MRI revealed what the doctors had suspected. Jenna had been born with a rare and devastating neurological disorder called Sturge-Weber Syndrome (SWS). This little-known disorder causes abnormal blood vessels to develop in the skin, eyes, and on the surface of the brain, and was the underlying cause of the port-wine birthmark on Jenna's face and the glaucoma in her right eye. Yet, it was the abnormal blood vessels on the surface of her brain that posed the greatest threat because they often lead to other health complications, including seizures, strokes and stroke-like episodes, impaired motor coordination, paralysis, developmental delays, learning disabilities, mental retardation, migraines, mood and behavior problems and, in some cases, even death.

During those early years, Jenna exhibited none of the problems associated with brain involvement. However, the glaucoma in her right eye was very serious and put her vision at risk. Just weeks after her birth, Jenna had to have surgery on her right eye in an effort to lower the eye's intraocular pressure. Unfortunately, the procedure didn't work, and a month later Jenna was back under anesthesia as the ophthalmologist attempted to implant a medical shunt in her eye to drain the fluid and release the escalating pressure. Although that procedure appeared to be a success, within months scar tissue clogged the shunt, leading to a series of follow-up procedures to clean out the shunt and ensure it was working properly.

During one such procedure, Jenna had an adverse reaction to the anesthesia and suffered a stroke-like episode. That frightening ordeal left Jenna with significant weakness in her left arm and left leg along with loss of motor coordination. Although in time she regained use of her arm and leg, the ordeal was a harbinger of things to come. Complications during subsequent surgical procedures caused other severe issues and problems, including retina detachment and loss of vision. Sadly, Jenna is now legally blind in her right eye and, with that eye, can see little more than shadows.

A couple of months after Jenna's 2nd birthday, the severity of the brain involvement became apparent. While my sister and her family were on vacation in Ocean City, Maryland, Jenna suffered the first of a wave of seizures, and was rushed to the Emergency Room at the local hospital. Doctors there had little experience with SWS and were unable to get the seizures under control. Before long, Jenna was transferred to the Pediatric Intensive Care Unit (PICU) at Johns Hopkins Hospital in Baltimore.

Over the next two weeks, despite around-the-clock efforts and the use of two anti-seizure medications, clusters of debilitating seizures ravaged Jenna's developing brain and fragile little body. In addition, Jenna had terrible reactions to the medications being administered, which brought on extreme agitation, disorientation, and hallucinations. At one point Jenna wasn't even able to recognize her own mother. I remember being in the PICU trying to comfort my poor little niece as she lay helpless, and wondering if this unhinged mental state was where she would forever remain. We could do little but look and pray the seizures would stop and Jenna would return to us.

The doctors then tried a third anti-seizure medication and indicated that if they couldn't get the seizures under control within the next 24 hours, they would look to perform a Hemispherectomy. This major surgical procedure involves disabling or removing the affected portion of the brain. It is an option of last resort when all else has failed. Thankfully, it didn't come to that. After pleas to family and friends for prayers, Jenna's seizures started to subside and eventually stopped. In time, she regained her mental acuity and physical strength.

Since shortly after her birth and to the present day, Jenna has been in the care of Anne Comi, M.D., one of the nation's leading SWS doctors. Dr. Comi is the Director of the Hunter Nelson Sturge-Weber Center at Kennedy Krieger Institute, an internationally recognized medical facility dedicated to the diagnosis, research, and treatment of SWS. Since the late 1990s, Dr. Comi has been treating SWS patients and researching the disorder, research that has yielded significant results.

Notwithstanding the progress Dr. Comi and her team have made, because SWS is so rare (affecting only 1 in 20,000 individuals) funding for SWS research and treatment programs has been difficult to obtain. Recognizing the need and importance of raising private funds, my sister Ida decided early on that she was going to do everything she could to help. So, despite Jenna's uncertain future and the inevitable challenges ahead, Ida set out to organize a charitable event that would create awareness and raise funds for research and treatment. It was her will and determination as well as Jenna's plight that inspired the rest of our family to get involved.

The plan was to create a fun and exciting charitable event at a scenic outdoor venue that showcased one of our home state's greatest assets, the Chesapeake Bay.

After much deliberation, we came up with the idea to host a concert and auction fundraiser, and we chose a picturesque waterfront site for its location. Since the event would feature bands playing on the shores of the Chesapeake Bay, we aptly named it *Bands on the Bay*.

Lots of hard work by an amazing group of dedicated family members and friends went into planning and preparations. And when that beautiful spring day in April of 2006 came, an army of volunteers helped make it a fun-filled and memorable event. Throughout the day, attendees were treated to rocking performances by great bands, an animated live auction conducted by a wisecracking, cowboy-hat-wearing auctioneer, and rousing speeches by Governor Robert Ehrlich and Congressman Steny Hoyer of Maryland. By day's end, *Bands on the Bay*, through loyal and generous support, proved to be a huge success, raising over $140,000 for the Hunter Nelson Sturge-Weber Center.

The success of the fundraiser motivated our family to turn *Bands on the Bay* into an annual event. Over the years, it has featured many great musical performances and guest appearances by notable professional athletes, including 9-time NFL Pro Bowler and Super Bowl Champion Alan Faneca, World Heavyweight Boxing Champion Riddick Bowe, and NFL Super Bowl Champion Rick "Doc" Walker.

Since the inaugural event, *Bands on the Bay* has raised over $1,000,000 for the Hunter Nelson Sturge-Weber Center and united thousands of people in the fight against SWS. These funds have directly supported the development of new strategies to reduce brain injury and other adverse effects of the disorder, provided treatment for patients without medical insurance, and helped fund research that led to the discovery of the cause of SWS.

According to Dr. Comi and the other senior authors of the clinical research that produced the discovery: Jonathan Pevsner, Ph.D., Professor in the Department of Neurology at Kennedy Krieger Institute, and Douglas A. Marchuk, Ph.D., Director of Molecular Genetics and Microbiology at Duke University School of Medicine, SWS and port-wine birthmarks are caused by a somatic activating mutation in the *GNAQ* gene. "This is a complete game changer for those with Sturge-Weber Syndrome and the millions born with port-wine birthmarks," said Dr. Comi. "Now that we know the underlying genetic mutation responsible for both conditions, we're hopeful that we can move quickly towards targeted therapies, offering families the promise of new treatments for the first time." Although much more research must be done, the study, published on May 8, 2013 in the *New England Journal of Medicine*, brings researchers closer than ever to a cure. "This is a giant step forward," said Dr. Comi. "We have real hope in the next five to ten years, perhaps sooner, perhaps a little longer, that there will be ... new treatments and perhaps even a cure for Sturge-Weber Syndrome."

Even with the success of *Bands on the Bay*, I couldn't help but think that there was more we could do to further the efforts to find a cure. More *I could do*. My desire to help Jenna live a better life started the wheels turning (well, not literally ... not just yet). Over the next few months, I toyed with several ideas for spreading the word about SWS to a broader audience and raising additional funds for ongoing research. I figured the best way to do it was to create a fundraiser that was both eye opening and inspiring. After mulling over different concepts, the wild idea to bicycle across America was born.

I envisioned a solo 3,000-mile ride from the Pacific Ocean in Santa Monica, California to the Atlantic in Ocean City, Maryland. The problem was – I had never been much of an athlete and wasn't really into biking (or "cycling" as those in the know call it). Actually, I wasn't into "cycling" *at all,* and didn't even own a bike. I knew if my cross-country journey was to become a reality, I would need a tremendous amount of help. So, before committing to the endeavor, I spoke to my immediate family and a handful of close friends to gauge their level of interest in helping. Most of those conversations began with questions like, "Are you kidding me?" or comments like, "You're crazy!" However, for the most part, everyone was very supportive.

I then reached out to experienced cyclists, medical professionals, and fitness/nutrition experts for advice. I needed to know what I'd be up against. Great advice, recommendations, and plenty of warnings followed. The particulars of it all were overwhelming (to say I'm a novice about these things would be a colossal understatement), but what I took from those talks was that, with proper training and careful planning, I could pull it off.

During that time, I was staying in Southern California in a beach town outside of Los Angeles. Although the surf and sunshine make for great training grounds, I didn't yet own a bicycle, so my training was limited to a stationary bike in a gym. (Laughable, I know, but it was the best I could do.) The months that followed could be described as exploratory at best. Although I believed I could bike across America, I needed to make sure my body was up to the challenge. I also needed to figure out how best to turn this crazy idea into a real and credible fund-raising and awareness-creating event.

Although it didn't happen overnight, in time I started to build up my strength and endurance and to gain confidence in myself physically (2 ½ hours a day on a stationary bike will do that for you). Also, a detailed plan for how to structure and promote the ride came together. I then reached out to potential sponsors and donors to let them know what I was planning to do. Before long, companies and individuals began pledging their support. With a final blessing from Ida, I set a start date (September 8, 2013) and the announcement was made. In that moment, my wild idea to bike across the country was transformed into a bona fide charitable event known as *Crossing America For A Cure*.

A few weeks before my departure, I purchased a green-and-white Novara Randonee bicycle and all the cycling essentials, suited up in a pair of bike shorts and a screaming yellow jersey, and nervously pedaled off for my first ride. (Nothing like waiting 'til the last minute, huh?) I wasn't equipped to navigate the mean streets of L.A. (or any streets for that matter), so my training rides took place on the Marvin Braude Bike Trail (aka the Strand), a 22-mile paved path that runs along the Pacific Ocean from Torrance to Pacific Palisades. Those last-minute rides were in essence a crash course in cycling, replete with crashes.

Novara Randonee on the Strand in Santa Monica, CA.

Despite my utter lack of experience (toppling over because I couldn't get my feet out of the clipless pedals was a daily occurrence) and lack of know-how (the art of changing a tire was a mystery to me), I knew that with a cure for SWS within reach, my cross-country bike ride had the potential to make a difference. As its name implies, *Crossing America For A Cure* is far more than just a fundraiser. It's a way to create awareness, a way to inspire others to join the fight against SWS, a way to give hope to Jenna and all those suffering with this devastating disorder. And it's a way to further the efforts to find a cure.

Al DeCesaris

Al DeCesaris at Will Rogers State Beach in Pacific Palisades, CA.

What follows is a daily account of Al DeCesaris' *Crossing America For A Cure* bicycle journey.

# Day 1 (9/8/13): Santa Monica, CA to Santa Clarita, CA [45 miles]

What an amazing day! Things couldn't have gone better (well, minus one roadside hiccup). It all started with a quick dip – well, more like a few ankle-deep steps – in the Pacific Ocean and a celebratory send-off at the Santa Monica Pier. My cousin Sonny Sukalo led the charge with motivational signs and T-shirts, and a homemade cake. Also there, cheering me on, were my friends Michel and John Wall, their daughter Kennedy, Heather, Sarah, John, Lauren, Jeff, Stephen, Stacy, and Randy (and her playful Boxer Roxy). We all had a great time together as we joked and posed for the camera.

Lauren Whiteley, Jeff Hollman, Randy Colonomos, Al DeCesaris, Sonny Sukalo, John Jameson, Heather McPeak, Sarah Graham at Santa Monica Pier in Santa Monica, CA (photo courtesy of Sukalo).

After the standard group photo and the proverbial "fun one," I made sure to get a shot in front of one of the Route 66 signs at the pier. The Santa Monica Pier is the symbolic ending point of the historic old route (the actual terminus is a few blocks away). Since I would be riding numerous miles on "The Mother Road" during my journey, I figured a picture in front of a Route 66 sign at the start of it all was in order.

Al DeCesaris and John Wall at Santa Monica Pier in Santa Monica, CA
(photo courtesy of Sonny Sukalo).

When I finally pedaled off – nervously, I must admit – John Wall was at my side. He knows the area well and led me safely out of Santa Monica and through the Los Angeles Westside. Good thing he was with me because if I had followed the route I had mapped out I would have been biking through the chaotic and congested heart of the city most of the day (and a few of its unsavory neighborhoods). That alone earned him a *Crossing America For A Cure* cycling jersey like the one I was wearing: it's red, white, and blue with the event logo emblazoned on the front and back.

Also accompanying me was a local man named Brian Allman. Brian learned about my ride from a news article in the *Santa Monica Patch* and decided he wanted to support the cause by riding some miles with me. It was incredible that this man, whom I had never met, gave of his time and energy to help. It was also exciting to know that our message was already getting out.

I'd like to say my handful of rides on the pedestrian-friendly Strand along the Pacific Ocean had me fully prepared for this adventure, but after the first big incline leading to the Sepulveda Pass I realized I was ill prepared for road riding with speeding cars and hills. Just before reaching the Sepulveda Boulevard Tunnel, Brian imparted a few words of wisdom, wished me well, and headed off. John and I then passed through the dimly lit tunnel before descending into the San Fernando Valley and the stifling valley heat.

A couple of hours later, as we rode along Sierra Highway through Canyon Country, back-to-back difficult climbs and the scorching high temperatures got the best of me. I had to stop, and took refuge on the side of the road under a tree as fatigue and dehydration (and doubt) set in. Fortunately for me, John is both a medical doctor and an experienced cyclist. He offered me water, energy chews, medical advice, and encouragement, which helped me regain my strength and my confidence. Before long, I was back in the saddle – the bike saddle, that is.

Not long after, John and I met up with his wife Michel and their daughter Kennedy for lunch. After eating, John and Michel asked if they could look through my panniers: the two neon yellow waterproof bags mounted on my bike rack. It was clear to them that I had grossly over-packed. They went through both of the panniers and pulled out a bunch of unnecessary things that were weighing me down. Apparently, jeans and collared shirts don't fall under the category of cycling essentials.

We then said our goodbyes and I continued on. I followed the highway northeast another 15 miles or so, just enough to get comfortable riding by myself. The solo biking proved manageable, but my surroundings caught me by surprise. The area was undeveloped and bleak; a drastic change from what I'd experienced hours before.

As the sun was sinking toward the horizon, I came across the Sierra Pelona Motel and a neighboring French restaurant, Le Chêne. For bicycling down a lonely road, *all alone*, this was a lucky find. While eating a delicious pasta dinner and downing about 10 glasses of ice water, I had the pleasure of meeting a wonderful couple. Their interest in our cause and their support of my efforts left me amazed (yet again) by the kindness of strangers.

I also received heartfelt messages and phone calls throughout the day from family and friends. The support and encouragement was nothing short of amazing. Even though I'm only 45 miles into this 3,000+ mile cross-country bicycle journey, I realize how difficult it's going to be. It's this support and encouragement that will give me the strength I need to make my journey a success.

Al DeCesaris on the beach in Santa Monica, CA (photo courtesy of Sonny Sukalo).

# Day 2 (9/9/13): Santa Clarita, CA to Apple Valley, CA [71 miles]

The training wheels are off, as they say. On Day 1, I had the good fortune of having experienced cyclists start me off on the first leg of my journey. Now, I'm heading down the open road with nothing but the sun and the stars to guide my way. Just kidding. I actually have several map and cycling apps on my phone, as well as my family back home navigating the route. With all that support, you'd think there wouldn't be problems, but even the most efficient systems have their glitches. I left the motel headed in the right direction, but soon lost my bearings and became unsure which way I should go. It took time to figure things out and work the kinks out of our system, but by noon I was back on course.

View from Sierra Hwy near Acton, CA.

This part of Los Angeles County is nothing like downtown L.A. or the beach towns along the coast. This is what is known as "high desert" with blistering heat and an arid landscape, making bicycle travel onerous. But it is also home to good, hardworking people willing to help. I experienced that first-hand when I stopped at a roadside fruit stand and met Denise. She welcomed me with a warm smile and sent me off with words of encouragement, refilled water bottles, and a free bag of fresh peaches.

Later in the day, as I rode through a rather desolate area and the "high desert" heat was taking its toll on me, the iTunes app on my phone somehow turned itself on. Pumping through my ear-buds was one of my favorite Rolling Stones songs, "Gimme Shelter." I don't know how it turned on, but with the sun beating down on me no song could have been more fitting at that moment.

View from Pierblossom Hwy near Llano, CA.

Despite the intense heat, Day 2 ended on a high note. Through *Warm Showers*, an organization that fosters hospitality exchange for touring cyclists, my sister Ida found a man willing to host me for the night. When I arrived at his house in Apple Valley (which rests in the southwest portion of San Bernardino County), I had the pleasure of meeting John McFarland, a real-life road angel. John welcomed me into his home, treated me to dinner, and imparted the knowledge he gained from his five – that's right, five! – bike tours across America. Like my friend John Wall the previous day, John McFarland made sure to help me as much as he could so that my journey would be a success.

Tomorrow off to Barstow. Now, off to bed.

# Day 3 (9/10/13): Apple Valley, CA to Barstow, CA [41 miles]

It was a productive morning. John McFarland took me to a local bike shop and a hardware store to get needed supplies for my journey. It seems I packed all the wrong things; but come on now, what were you expecting? It's not like I go on cross-country bike trips all the time. Thanks to his years of experience, John was able to get me fitted out for the long, arduous journey, and off I went.

Not long after my riding day began, my road angel pulled up next to me in his truck to give me a couple of valve adapters he had just bought for me. The adapters enable Presta valves to accept Schrader valve pumps, which would allow me to inflate my bike tires at gas station pumps should the need arise. The adapters were something I should have had (or at least known about), but, as I'm sure you're starting to realize, my cycling knowledge leaves a lot to be desired. John explained exactly what they were and how to use them. It was yet another good deed by a good man.

In the early afternoon, I turned onto historic Route 66 – formally known as "Will Rogers Highway" and informally as "Main Street of America" or "The Mother Road" – toward the city of Barstow. The old road was established in the 1920s and originally ran 2,448 miles from Chicago, Illinois through Missouri, Kansas, Oklahoma, Texas, New Mexico, and Arizona before reaching its western terminus in Santa Monica, California. It served as a major path for those migrating west and, for a time, was arguably the most famous road in America before the Interstate Highway System replaced it.

I've heard there's a certain romance about traveling the famous old route, but this stretch that runs through the Mojave Desert is a sad, lonely road. Homes and businesses that had once flourished during Route 66's glory days are now boarded-up and abandoned, mere remnants of what once was. The road itself isn't in much better shape than the derelict structures that plague it. It's in overall disrepair with a crumbling shoulder, 24 inches wide (at best).

View from National Trails Hwy (Rt 66) near Helendale, CA.

Although it was a relatively short ride to Barstow, the sun was blazing hot and the landscape was bleak and desolate, making the journey difficult. As I struggled along, I noticed two vultures circling overhead ominously. Although at times I lost sight of them, I don't think they were ever far off. It was as though they remained with me, mile after painful mile, just waiting for me to keel over.

When I finally arrived in Barstow, my cell phone went dead, which presented a problem because the address of the motel I was to stay in was in my phone. Unsure of where to go, I stopped at a convenience store to see if someone could help me. There I met Grace, one of the store employees, who offered me a map and allowed me to charge my phone. I told her about our cause and about Jenna. She was taken by my endeavor and very supportive of what we are trying to accomplish. She mentioned her granddaughter Serena, who suffers with leukemia. Like Jenna, Serena's life is filled with many challenges. Love and support are essential for her well-being as it is for all children suffering with such diseases.

With my phone charged, I was able to retrieve the address of the motel and located it soon after. The accommodations were clean and safe, and as luck would have it located right across the street from a pizza parlor. A hand-tossed brick-oven pizza later, I returned to my motel room and retired for the night one very happy man.

# Day 4 (9/11/13): Barstow, CA to Ludlow, CA [53 miles]

Last spring, I drove along Interstate 40 as I made my way to southern California from my home state of Maryland. It was a scenic drive that I hoped to make again one day. Yet, I never envisioned doing it on a bicycle.

Although riding a bike on an interstate comes with its share of challenges, it also comes with some distinct advantages. One in particular is interstates are straight (relatively speaking), making I-40, as I travel east across California, the most direct route. Another advantage is the wide shoulder, which is often wider than the lanes of the interstate. Yet, probably the biggest advantage is if a problem should arise, there are plenty of people driving by who could come to your aid. That is especially important for someone (a completely inexperienced someone) traveling solo through the Mojave Desert on a human-powered, pizza-fueled bike.

I'd be remiss, though, if I didn't mention a couple of the disadvantages of interstate bicycle riding. Take those seemingly benign cuts in the pavement known as "rumble strips" for instance. They may be a legitimate safety feature for drifting vehicles, but they're definitely no friend of a bicycle. Whenever I ride over them my front tire bounces violently, and it feels like I'm working a jackhammer as I struggle to keep my bike steady. Another disadvantage is roadwork. I realize it usually leads to frustrating delays for vehicles, but it creates a whole host of problems for someone on a bicycle; particularly when the roadwork is taking place on the shoulder I'm biking on. As I've now seen, there's plenty of danger on both sides of those orange cones.

View from I-40 near Ludlow, CA.

In the early afternoon, I stopped at a rest area to pick up food and drinks. Unfortunately, this particular rest area (which was one of the only ones I saw the entire day) had no restaurants, mini-marts, or even a vending machine. To top it off, their public water fountains were out of service. Lucky for me, a grounds maintenance worker named Mike allowed me to fill my water bottles from the staff's water supply. While there, I also met Dannie and Dominic from England, who are on vacation touring the southwest (yet unlike me, they're doing it by way of an air-conditioned car). I told them about Jenna and about our efforts to create awareness and raise funds. They were enthused and excited to support the cause.

Soon after, I returned to the road and continued on to the desert town of Ludlow, which rests just off of I-40 in the heart of San Bernardino County. From what I learned, the "original" Ludlow is a tumbleweed-ridden ghost town located to the south (along Route 66), though the "new" Ludlow I rolled into wasn't much livelier. It's little more than a way station with a few businesses that cater to people traveling along the interstate. Its one motel is a dilapidated one-story building with eight rooms and no reception area. The front desk (if you will) is the checkout counter inside the gas station mini-mart across the street. No joke. I literally had to go inside the mini-mart to check-in and pick up my room key.

Outside of the mini-mart, I had the pleasure of meeting Kelly Slater. No, not Kelly Slater, the World Surfing Champion. This was Kelly Slater, the pastor from Santa Rosa, California. Kelly was so moved by our cause, as well as by Jenna's story, that he prayed with me for my safety and for Jenna's health. I was touched by his admiration for what we are trying to achieve and his genuine concern for our well-being. It was a powerful and humbling experience.

The night ended on a rather funny note when John and Michel Wall called to see how I was doing. They'd been tracking my progress through the website *MapMyRide*, and apparently the site showed that I had been going in small circles in the middle of the desert.

Their first thought was that I must be suffering from dehydration and was delirious. Although hours of biking through the Mojave Desert did do a number on me, what I was actually doing was filming myself pedaling down the road with my GoPro camera set on a tripod. It took a number of passes to get this one particular shot right, and that must have been what made them think I was pedaling around in aimless circles. Dehydrated maybe, delirious not yet, but there's still plenty more desert riding to come.

Al DeCesaris in Ludlow, CA (photo courtesy of Kelly Slater).

# Day 5 (9/12/13): Ludlow, CA to Needles, CA [93 miles]

So, this was the big one. Maybe the longest ride of the entire journey (and, most likely, the hottest): 90+ miles to the city of Needles. I'd been told this part of California can get blazing hot, even in September. Lucky for me, the forecast for the day was rather mild. Keep in mind, it was still in the high 90s, so obviously "mild" is a relative term.

With temps like this, hydration is vital. Therefore, I made every effort to carry as much water as I could, even going so far as dumping some clothing to make room in my panniers for additional water bottles. It seemed to add an extra 10 pounds, but it was weight I was more than willing to carry.

Before leaving town, I met two guys who were on their way to Santa Fe, New Mexico. They were both shocked and excited when they heard that I was biking across the country by myself. While we were chatting, they noticed that the pressure in my back tire was low and pointed it out to me. They then helped me pump up the tire before heading out.

The mountain vistas along Interstate 40 were a sight to behold. It's surprising how a land that can be so harsh and inhospitable can be so beautiful at the same time.

Yet, this part of southern California clearly holds that power. Despite the grueling nature of the day's ride, the sheer beauty of the landscape made it all worthwhile.

View from I-40 near Amboy, CA.

At roughly the halfway point, I took a break at a rest area (one with working water fountains this time) near the community of Essex. I met several people there, including a guy named Randy who offered me fresh fruit and a cold drink. Again, I found myself astounded at how kind and supportive people have been toward me.

However, the problem-free day was not to last. While leaving the rest area, I had to hit the brakes to avoid a curb. I was unable to unclip my foot from the pedal in time and toppled over. Fortunately, I didn't get hurt and sprang to my feet, but the fall did not go unnoticed. A grounds maintenance worker, with a look of concern on his face, asked if I was all right. "I'm okay. It happens sometimes," I responded nonchalantly as though it was an everyday occurrence. Admittedly, it kind of is. Since I bought the bike a little over a month ago, this was probably the 15th time I'd fallen.

The remainder of the ride included a long steady climb before a steep descent into Needles, which rests on the western bank of the Colorado River. The shoulder on I-40 outside of the city was a disaster. It was beset with cracked pavement and covered with debris. Navigating the sharp downward slope while bouncing and swerving made for a daunting ride those last few miles.

When I got there, I went to a restaurant called the Wagon Wheel for a hard-earned meal. For whatever reason, I've been craving breakfast food (pancakes, waffles, home fries and such) since I set out on this journey, and little roadside restaurants like this seem to fit the bill. Once my plate of eggs and home fries was wiped clean, the waitress approached my table with the check. However, I wasn't quite finished, and asked her to bring back the menu so I could have another look. The waitress looked at me like I was joking, but when I ordered another plate of food, she knew I was serious. In no time flat, I inhaled a stack of pancakes smothered in maple syrup and a side of bacon. Ah, the benefits of burning 5,000 calories a day.

# Day 6 (9/13/13): Needles, CA to Kingman, AZ [57 miles]

I had been looking forward to this day for some time. The day's ride would mark the completion of my first state and, hopefully, the first of many such accomplishments in my journey across America.

Although the weather was dreadfully hot and I was a bit weary after all the miles I covered yesterday, I left Needles feeling pretty good. The morning ride went well and, just before 1:00 pm, I crossed the Colorado River and entered "The Grand Canyon State." Like a typical camera-wielding tourist, I broke out my iPhone and GoPro camera and shot a slew of photos and video in front of the Arizona sign. I then celebrated my achievement as though I'd just won the Super Bowl.

Al DeCesaris in front of the Arizona sign on I-40 near Topock, AZ.

It was an awesome feeling to know that I had biked across an entire state. Prior to this journey, I never would have dreamed I could do such a thing. The fact of the matter is, it wouldn't have been possible without Jenna inspiring me, or without the help, support, and encouragement of so many people.

The Colorado River and the Needles from I-40 near Topock, AZ.

Not long after, I spotted a leafy tree on the side of Interstate 40 (which, in this arid region, isn't a common sight), and stopped to have lunch in the shade. Despite the rapid succession of tractor-trailers, cars, and motorcycles whizzing by, my roadside picnic was rather pleasant. I think I was just happy to be out of the hot sun for a while and to be sitting on something other than my bike seat. Still, next time I'll need to remember to pack a better variety of food and drinks. Clif Bars and water just aren't as exciting as they used to be.

Despite my efforts to make decent time, I ended up having to pedal like a wild man the last couple of hours to reach my destination of Kingman, Arizona prior to sundown. As though the situation wasn't stressful enough, right before reaching Kingman, I encountered a steep, twisting climb just as the shoulder narrowed, leaving me dangerously close to a metal guardrail on one side and speeding traffic on the other. It was a harrowing and rigorous ride, to say the least.

Since the motel my family booked was several miles past the restaurants in town, my sister Ida recommended that I stop to get something to eat before heading to the motel. Needless to say, after another long day on the road and my frantic race against the setting sun, I was almost as excited to see a Cracker Barrel as I was the Arizona state line. Then again, when I'm hungry, I'm always excited to see a Cracker Barrel!

# Day 7 (9/14/13): Kingman, AZ to Kingman, AZ [25 miles]

Yep, you read that right. I started my day in Kingman and ended it there. Thanks to a slow leak in my back tire in the morning and two successive flats in the afternoon, I ended up having to turn back before my day really got going. Although I hated having to pedal back to Kingman, it was the wise thing to do since Seligman, my next destination, was still 60+ miles away. Continuing on after all the time lost from dealing with the slow leak and the two flats would have left me out on Interstate 40 hours after sundown. On a bicycle, with no streetlights overhead, a busy interstate wasn't a place I cared to be. So when the day was done, I had biked 25 miles round trip with nothing to show for it except two punctured bike tubes and grease under my fingernails.

It was bound to happen, I suppose. It wasn't as if I was going to bike 3,000+ miles without facing problems. And, as Ida pointed out, as far as bike trouble goes, I was very fortunate. When the first flat occurred, I was able to get John Wall on the phone to walk me through the tire-changing process. (Yes, when in doubt, I phone a friend.) The second flat happened not long after, and within sight of a service station. There, the manager lent me a pair of needle-nose pliers and a firefighter helped me remove the small jagged piece of metal that caused the flats. It appeared to be a wire filament from a blown-out steel-belted radial tire, remnants of which littered the rocky shoulder of the interstate. Like the goathead (those spiky plant seeds that are said to cause flats), they're a common and ruthless enemy of bicycle tires.

Had this occurred farther down the road, I would have been in big trouble because there aren't any service stations or rest areas along I-40 till you reach Seligman. Riding a heavy steel-frame bike with over 50 pounds of gear is difficult enough; pushing it all that way would have been a nightmare.

Despite the day's setbacks, I learned some valuable lessons (namely, how to change a tire) and was reminded yet again that when one is in need of help, there are people willing to lend a hand. Since this journey began, I've been in need several times, and each time I've been blessed to receive the help necessary to continue on. So flat tires or what have you, I intend to do just that.

Novara Randonee with a flat tire on I-40 near Kingman, AZ.

# Day 8 (9/15/13): Kingman, AZ to Seligman, AZ [87 miles]

Back on the road. This time with air in my tires. The original plan was to take Interstate 40 to Seligman. But the terrible condition of the shoulder, and a sense of foreboding (that this stretch of the interstate, which had already caused two flat tires, would cause another) called for a change in plans. So, despite the fact that the alternate along Route 66 was about 15 miles longer, I decided to follow the famous old road and tackle the extra miles.

This stretch of "The Mother Road" was much more scenic than the one I rode on in the Mojave Desert and proved to be far livelier. At one roadside store, I met a woman named CJ who expressed great interest in our cause. Later in the day, I met Tim and several others at the Hackberry General Store. The store was like a Disney re-creation of Route 66 in its heyday, replete with road memorabilia, old-fashioned soda machines and gas pumps, and a red '57 Chevrolet Corvette convertible parked out front. Tim had kind words and well wishes for me. He also gave me his business card and told me that if I had any problems while passing through his home state of Oklahoma to give him a call. After the trouble I had yesterday, I didn't need to be told twice. Should problems arise, I'll take him up on that offer. I just hope he knows how to change a bicycle tire better than I do.

View from Rt 66 near Hackberry, AZ.

Not far down the road, Route 66 snaked between rocky outcrops and low mountains that looked as though they wore crowns. The rugged, lifeless terrain then started to give way to the green of grass and shrubs and the occasional golden-yellow of Black-Eyed Susans. It seemed to be the point where two competing worlds melded together, making for one spectacular landscape.

View from Rt 66 near Hackberry, AZ.

A bit farther along, I stopped at the Hualapai Lodge in Peach Springs to take a break and get some water. The lodge is named after the Hualapai Indian Tribe (which is pronounced Wal-lah-pie and means "People of the Tall Pines") and is located on the Hualapai reservation. Although the lodge didn't have a place where I could get water myself, April, one of the employees, filled my water bottles and got me back on the road in short order.

In the early evening, I arrived in Seligman. After checking into my motel and taking a quick shower, I headed over to the Roadkill Cafe for a bite to eat. As you can imagine, the name of the establishment raised some doubts, but it was right next door to the motel and I was hungry, *real hungry;* so I decided to give it a go. Plus, I figured if you're confident enough to have a slogan like "You Kill It – We Grill It," and include dishes like Deer Delectables, Bad-Brake Steak, and Fender Tenders on your menu, your food has to be good. I was happy to learn that it actually was.

On my way back to my room, I was greeted by motel neighbors Dirk and Gisela from Germany, and invited over for a cold beverage. They had seen me biking down the road earlier and wanted to hear about my adventures. Even though beer wasn't on "The Nutrition Plan" my fitness and health expert Lauren Majewski put together for me, I figured *one* wouldn't hurt. (Sorry, Lauren, it had to be done.) The way I look at it, after biking 80+ miles, my body needed the calories and the carbs.

# Day 9 (9/16/13): Seligman, AZ to Flagstaff, AZ [80 miles]

If the ride to Needles was the "big one," this was the "tough one." Eighty miles made up largely of climb, after climb – one steeper than the next. Needless to say, it wasn't fun … and it sure wasn't pretty. (Well, the mountain vistas and the Ponderosa Pines were.) Adding to my difficulties, the bicycle chain kept slipping out of the higher gears. I'm not sure when this started to happen because I don't often shift into those gears, but I suspect I did something to cause the problem when I changed the back tire (twice) outside of Kingman.

View from I-40 near Williams, AZ.

Once the worst of the climbs were behind me (or, more accurately, below me), I took a much-needed breather in Williams. Williams is a quaint little city with an Old West feel and Route 66 charm. There, I met a lady named Lydia and spoke to her about our efforts and the importance of raising awareness about Sturge-Weber Syndrome. She seemed genuinely interested in our cause and told me to reach out to her should I need anything when passing through her hometown of Albuquerque. It's awesome how perfect strangers can be so caring.

Later in the day, I spoke on the phone with one of my childhood best friends, Bob Stanger. From the start, Bob has been a loyal and generous supporter of the cause and has even offered to ride with me on the back end of my journey as I make my way through Maryland. As he always does, Bob offered encouragement and great advice. He also had thoughts on why the chain was slipping, but without seeing the bicycle firsthand, he couldn't be certain of the problem. He recommended that I take it into a bike shop to have it inspected.

After a bit more climbing (which topped out at an elevation of 7,335 feet), I began my approach into Flagstaff while Ida worked on finding a bike repair shop for me. Coincidentally, Flagstaff is a bicycle-friendly city and has many quality bike shops. She decided on Absolute Bikes because it was close to where I was staying for the night and, more important, they could get me in on short notice.

Although several different employees helped me, one in particular named Kyle took the lead and adjusted the derailleur so the chain wouldn't slip anymore. (It seems someone, *this someone* to be exact, tightened the limiting screws too much and caused the problem.) Kyle also fitted my bike with new tires after an inspection revealed that the back tire was severely worn down. Apparently, the weight of all the gear I'm carrying on the rack was too much for the standard tires that came with the bike. Who'd have thought 50+ pounds of gear would be too much weight? Obviously, not this cycling novice.

Leaving Absolute Bikes a satisfied customer, I headed to the home of Cynthia McKinnon and Elson Miles (my hosts for the night), whom Ida found through *Warm Showers*. I was welcomed into their home like an old friend and, within minutes of my arrival, a feast was set before me. The day's adventures ended with good music, great food, and even better company.

View from Rt 66 near Seligman, AZ.

# Day 10 (9/17/13): Flagstaff, AZ to Holbrook, AZ [91 miles]

The day started with a farewell to Elson, as he headed to Las Vegas for a bike show, and a leisurely breakfast with Cynthia. We ate and sipped coffee and discussed the current events in Arizona and the country at large. When the meal was finished – and we were contented we had solved all of the nation's problems – I packed my gear and headed out. Although I'm fairly certain I won't be biking across America again anytime soon, next time I pass through Flagstaff I'll definitely pay my new friends a visit. Their hospitality was a real treat.

As I pedaled off, I noticed that my breathing was markedly strained. I suppose it was to be expected – Flagstaff sits at just over 6,900 feet above sea level, and my training rides (the few that I did) took place at sea level (literally, at the seashore). Thus, the air was much thinner than I was used to. Still, the ride away from the city was relatively easy. The majority of it was downhill, allowing me to relax as I coasted on my new thicker, wider tires – the highly-regarded Schwalbe Marathon Plus 700c x 38mm.

Around noon, I came upon an area with reddish-brown soil speckled with deep green vegetation. I had seen hints of this on previous days, but nothing as striking as this. Amid the wild landscape was a sign that read, "Next Rest Area 124 miles." After my initial shock and a moment of panic, I started to chuckle because Ida had made me aware of how far I needed to ride to reach my destination of Holbrook, and it was well short of the posted 124 miles. Still, call it neurotic behavior or what you will, I *had* to double-check the map on my phone to make certain. Just as I thought, Holbrook was another 60 miles or so down the road. It was a good thing too because if I'd had to bike another 124 miles, I probably would have ended up calling Cynthia for a roadside rescue.

View from I-40 near Winslow, AZ.

Although the weather forecast called for clear skies, in the early afternoon I rode through a patch of rain and gusting wind. It caught me by surprise and had me worried because, at one point, the rain was coming down hard and the wind was swirling and pushing me around. But as quickly as it had started up, it died down. It was as though there was one little storm cloud hovering over my path just to remind me to keep my guard up.

Later in the day, as I was riding past the city of Winslow, a red truck pulled onto the shoulder in front of me. I wasn't certain what the driver was doing, but when I saw the man's face I realized it was Tim, who I had met at the Hackberry General Store a couple of days back. Running into someone I know on the interstate was as hilarious as it was preposterous. As Tim and I spoke, we marveled and laughed at the sheer improbability of it. Things like that just don't happen every day.

As the day began to wind down, discomfort started to set in. There's a certain condition (which shall remain nameless) that cyclists often develop on their rears from too much riding. And there's a certain someone (who shall also remain nameless) who was falling victim to the condition. Needless to say, by the time that certain someone arrived in Holbrook, he was in bad shape.

Thankfully, one of my best friends from high school, Bryan Springer, is a medical doctor and knew exactly what was needed to treat the condition. Holbrook doesn't have much, but it has a pharmacy and they carried just what the doctor ordered. So when the day was done, I had another 90+ miles under my belt ... as well as some medicated comfort.

# Day 11 (9/18/13): Holbrook, AZ to Gallup, NM [94 miles]

Remember when I said that running into people you know on the interstate just doesn't happen every day? Well, guess what? I'm now starting to think it does. As I was riding on the shoulder of Interstate 40, a truck pulled over just ahead of me, and in it were Randy and Patti, whom I had met on Day 5 at a rest area outside of Essex, California. We talked for a few minutes and had a good laugh about running into each other again. Before we parted, Randy asked me if I needed anything, just as he had done the first time I saw him. Although I didn't need anything at the time, the kindness of my new friends did not go unnoticed.

Not long after, John Wall's sister Lisa Espelien and her husband Mark (who have been following my journey through our website) saw me pedaling down the interstate as they were driving from California to their home in Albuquerque. As we had yet to meet, they pulled over to introduce themselves and see how I was doing. The plan was to meet up with them in Albuquerque in a few days, but it was nice of them to stop and check in on me when they did – especially since they had an ice-cold Gatorade for me ... which, at the time, I desperately needed. FYI: If you see me biking down the road under a hot summer sun, a gift of fresh fruit or a cold drink will make me your friend for life.

As an aside, a question I keep getting asked is, "Where is your support vehicle?" Although I don't have a "SAG Wagon" following me with food and gear, I do have an incredible support team in my family back home and in all the other people who have been helping me, praying for me, and encouraging me along the way. From the start, the support I've received has been extraordinary – today's roadside visits were yet another example of that – and has made what I've achieved thus far possible.

In the late morning, I received a call from *Crossing America For A Cure* resident physical therapist John Gallagher. John just so happens to be one of my best friends from college and a pseudo-cyclist like myself. Although I was feeling pretty good during the day's ride, I had felt slight discomfort in my lower back earlier in the week. I realize some back discomfort is to be expected when you're leaning over handlebars all day long. Still, I thought it best to bring it to John's attention. He recommended various exercises and stretches to prevent things from getting worse. I hope it helps, though I'm sure by the time I reach Maryland I'll have pain and discomfort just about everywhere.

Although the tentative plan for the day was to bike 48 miles to Chambers, Arizona, the thought of crossing another state line had me eager to press on. Ida and I had previously discussed the possibility of bypassing Chambers and making for Gallup, New Mexico; thus, I knew what it meant mileage-wise – another punishing 90+ mile day. By the time I reached Chambers it was still early in the day and I was feeling good, so I phoned my family to let them know I was continuing on despite the additional miles.

View from I-40 near Lupton, AZ.

Around 2:00 pm, I entered Navajo Nation, a semi-autonomous territory governed by the Navajo Indian tribe. Dominated by rock formations of beige and sandy pink, and massive mesas of burnt sienna and cream, the land is both bizarre and beautiful. As I was riding and filming – yes, at the same time – the dazzling landscape, I came upon a sign that read, "Welcome to New Mexico. The Land of Enchantment." It was an awesome sight and filled me with a real sense of accomplishment. Before crossing into New Mexico, I held a "selfie photo shoot" and videoed myself doing some celebratory fist pumps. "Dance like nobody's watching," Mark Twain once said. I guess, in my own way, I did just that. And, who knows, when I cross into the next state, I just may do a little actual dancing.

Al DeCesaris in front of the New Mexico sign on I-40 near Gallup, NM.

View from I-40 near Gallup, NM.

# Day 12 (9/19/13): Gallup, NM to Grants, NM [69 miles]

For most of the day, I rode past mesas of tan, muted pink, and orangey-red flecked with vegetation of green as well as peculiar-looking rock formations that appeared as though they had been hewn by human hands. Like Arizona, New Mexico boasts a strange and wild landscape, making travel (even on an unforgiving leather bike saddle) captivating and enjoyable.

View from I-40 near Gallup, NM.

The shoulder through these parts, however, brought me no joy. It was as though someone took gravel and tried to clump it together with glue. And not Krazy Glue or something that actually works, it was more like that goopy white mess school children use that never seems to hold anything together. Come on, New Mexico, you can do better than that. Seriously though, it was one of the worst riding surfaces I've encountered. And to top it off (no pun intended), it was covered with swarms of little insects that seemed to pop up in the air like Mexican jumping beans. At first I thought they were cicada because I had heard that this is the year they are to return. But after getting a closer look at them, I started to think they were crickets … or grasshoppers. Who knows, maybe they were locusts. I suppose I should have paid more attention during science class. Whatever they were, they seemed to have made a home of Interstate 40's shoulder, just as I have.

In the early afternoon, I passed the Continental Divide of the Americas, which, according to Wikipedia, "separates the watersheds that drain into the Pacific Ocean from those river systems that drain into the Atlantic Ocean (including those that drain into the Gulf of Mexico and the Caribbean Sea)." Thanks, Wikipedia, for that succinct yet potentially flawed description. Despite the significance, I crossed the Continental Divide with little fanfare (well, none actually).

Later in the day, I received some exciting news. Alan Faneca, 9-time NFL Pro Bowler and Super Bowl Champion, announced that he will match all funds raised through *Crossing America For A Cure*! "Al's efforts are near to my heart since my daughter, Anabelle, has SWS as well," Alan Faneca stated. "So, let's all help Al on his journey for a cure. My family and I will match every dollar raised on his journey." Over the years, Alan and his wife Julie have generously supported our fundraising efforts, yet what they are doing for this event is extraordinary. As I pedaled toward the city of Grants (my destination for the day), I couldn't stop thinking what an honor it is to have such an amazing family standing with us in the fight against Sturge-Weber Syndrome.

View from I-40 near Thoreau, NM.

View from I-40 near Prewitt, NM.

# Day 13 (9/20/13): Grants, NM to Albuquerque, NM [85 miles]

The scenery was spectacular yet again. I started the day riding past mesas blanketed with rocks, grass, and shrubs among uplands that looked as though manmade fortresses were perched atop them. Not long after, I saw an odd yet fascinating outcrop of crumbling stone set against a backdrop of bright blue sky. Farther down the road, I was treated to muddy-red and orangey-pink rock formations and imposing rock walls that appeared to be rising from the ground on both sides of Interstate 40.

View from I-40 near New Laguna, NM.

View from I-40 near New Laguna, NM.

After several hours of steady riding, I pulled over to relieve myself. Oh, don't raise your eyebrows. When rest areas are hours apart, you do what you have to do. I am discreet about it if it makes you feel any better. Anyway, it was just a quick stop. When I returned to my bike, I noticed that there were hitchhikers (goatheads, I do believe) attached to my shoes and socks. I figured I could just brush them off; however, when I tried to, one of them stuck me in the thumb and index finger, turning my digits into pincushions. I hastily flicked it away and started sucking blood from the wounds and spitting it out as if a venomous snake had bitten me. I imagine people driving by must have had a good laugh. I know I did once I calmed down.

As I approached Albuquerque, I encountered a rise that was steep, high, and seemingly never-ending. Cycling experts say that pedaling from a seated position is the most efficient way to climb, but not far into it my legs began burning and I slowed to a crawl. So contrary to the opinions of the "experts," I lifted myself out of the saddle and started standing pedaling (as I often do). It may be inefficient, but it allows me to use my body weight to apply extra force to the pedals and seems to help me ascend more quickly. More important, it gives my butt a much-needed break. When I reached the crest, I was rewarded with breathtaking views of Albuquerque, the Rio Grande, and the Sandia Mountains in the distance.

Navigating the city itself proved breathtaking as well, though not for the same reason. I had been forewarned that biking on I-40 through Albuquerque would be difficult, and perhaps even dangerous. The alternate routes through and around the city, however, were confusing and long. So after conferring with Ida and good ole John McFarland, whom I'd met on Day 2, I decided to stay on the interstate and roll through the heart of the city.

Well, my confidence (or, shall we say, my naïveté) soon vanished when I realized what I was up against. There was heavy traffic across the entire roadway, exit ramps and merge lanes everywhere, and a massive interchange that had vehicles converging from all directions. Avoiding speeding cars and trucks was like playing a game of live-action Frogger. I realize I'm dating myself with that 80s arcade game reference, but it's the best way to describe the sheer madness of it all.

Despite the perilous ride, when the day was done, I'd managed to make it safely across Albuquerque, and saved both time and miles in the process.

# Day 14 (9/21/13): Albuquerque, NM to Santa Rosa, NM [108 miles]

In cycling terms, a bicycle ride of 100 miles or more within 12 hours is known as a "century ride." Now, I had completed three 90+ mile rides, but I had yet to top 100. However, today was to be the day, because, in order to reach Santa Rosa (my destination for the day), I would have to bike well over 100 miles.

Although the distance was daunting, the elevations weren't bad, and I was fortunate to have Mark Espelien ride with me for the first few hours of the day. If you recall, I met Mark and his wife Lisa on Day 11 while I was making my way to Gallup. Mark is an avid cyclist and knows the Albuquerque metro area well, so having him guide me around the Sandia Mountains was a big help.

We met at my motel in the morning and started out along Route 66 from there. After yesterday's chaotic experience, returning to "The Mother Road" (which is like a sleepy country road compared to Interstate 40) made for a calm and peaceful ride. It was also nice to have company, seeing as I hadn't ridden with anyone since the first day of the trip. Mark, however, may beg to differ because I talked his ear off the entire ride. I suppose I can get a little chatty after a couple of weeks of solitude.

Novara Randonee on Rt 66 in Moriarty, NM.

After we got down the road a ways and the terrain leveled out, Mark and I shook hands and said our goodbyes. I then got back onto I-40 and continued on toward Santa Rosa. Here's a fun (and useless) fact for you. Santa Rosa, along with Santa Monica and Santa

Clarita, is the third "Santa" city I've stopped in on my journey. Oh, the things you think about after 14 straight days on a bicycle.

Despite the pressure of having to cover 100+ miles before nightfall, I carved out a little time to eat at one of my favorite lunch spots ... which these days happens to be under an overpass. I know that sounds like a weird place to put up one's feet and have a bite to eat, but it's the ideal location when you're biking across the country and there's nothing between rest areas except miles upon miles of open road.

Several hours later, when Santa Rosa came into view, the sun was still surprisingly well above the horizon. Even more surprising, I was still pedaling strong with over 100 miles complete. Notching a century ride was super exciting, and for me a significant achievement. (Remember, I'm the cycling novice who put in just a handful of training rides before setting out on a 3,000+ mile bike ride.) And the realization that, with today's ride, I had reached the 1,000-mile mark (well, 999 miles according to Ida's calculations) made it all the sweeter.

I'm proud to say, I'm now approximately one-third of the way through my cross-country journey. Just another couple thousand miles to go....

# Day 15 (9/22/13): Santa Rosa, NM to Tucumcari, NM [62 miles]

The day began with a bit of a dilemma. As I rode down the on-ramp onto Interstate 40 I saw a sign that read, "Pedestrians and Bicycles Prohibited." This was the first time I had seen any restrictions of that sort. I immediately came to a stop and called Ida, my trusty navigator. Ida did a quick online search and determined that there was another road I could take. However, if I were to follow this alternate route, it would add considerable mileage to the day's ride and take much longer to reach my destination of Tucumcari. Despite my frustration, after much deliberation I walked my bike off the on-ramp, lifted it over the guardrail, and started making my way toward the alternate route.

Yet, as soon as I did, I came upon an old man walking down the road. I asked him if the alternate route was the best way to go. Without hesitation, he told me to ride my bike on I-40. "People do it all the time. The police don't care," he added, as though it was something everyone knew to be true.

Now, I've been biking I-40 almost every day since leaving Barstow, California and have yet to see anyone else riding a bicycle on the interstate, so who these "people" are that *do it all the time* I haven't a clue. Still, this random old man aimlessly walking down the road seemed to be a good enough authority for me. So back over the guardrail and onto the on-ramp I went, and down the shoulder of I-40 I rode.

Each night in preparation for the next day's ride, Ida provides me with detailed information on the route I'm to take, including directions, mileage, elevations, weather, and so forth. Her help with this has been a godsend. Without it, I'd be lost, literally and figuratively. One thing she indicated last night was that there was going to be 18 mph wind in the morning and early afternoon. Other than one instance several days back, I hadn't experienced strong wind and didn't know how it might affect me. Well, let me tell you, strong wind, as I'm now learning, can make riding very difficult and can even pose a real danger. The wind I faced today not only slowed my pace, a few times it even pushed me across the shoulder like tumbleweed and had me wrestling with the bike to keep it upright.

Adding to my frustrations, for some odd reason, iTunes kept playing song after song from the one Christmas carol album and the one classical music album I have on my phone. Okay, I recognize it's my own fault for having these songs in my music library, but during the holidays the carols serve their purpose, and every now and then the classical music comes in handy (like when I'm trying to fall asleep). After suffering through "Jingle Bells" and "Adagio for Strings" the umpteenth time, I started to think (actually, I became convinced) that iTunes was having a little fun with me.

In the late afternoon, I came across the most revolting creature known to man (well, at least to me) – the tarantula. And not just one little guy on the side of the road, but several humungous, nasty, hairy crawlers directly in my path, one after the other, over the course of a few miles. Even though I gave each of them a wide berth when I passed, I couldn't help but think that they had somehow leaped onto my bike and were just waiting to sink their fangs into me. After frantically brushing off my back for the tenth time, I realized I was letting my imagination (and my arachnophobia) get the best of me.

View from I-40 near Tucumcari, NM.

The one positive of the day's ride was the scenery, which was phenomenal. The strange muddy-red soil had returned only to be outdone by a stream of soupy muddy-red water. Mesas, low mountains, and rock formations of various hues of pink and red floated in seas of golden-green grass and the deep green of

Buffalo Juniper. As I travel farther east into the Great Plains, where the landscape will be vastly different, I begin to realize how much I'm going to miss the mesmerizing lands of America's Southwest.

View from I-40 near Tucumcari, NM.

# Day 16 (9/23/13): Tucumcari, NM to Dalhart, TX [94 miles]

The last few days have been filled with discussions about which route I should take as I move east into the Great Plains. The original plan was to ride into Colorado, then head east. However, severe rains in Colorado and the elevations of the Rocky Mountains made me re-think that. One possibility was to continue east on Interstate 40 to Oklahoma City, then start going northeast from there. Another was to stay on I-40 all the way to Tennessee, then head north. Despite our indecision, the route became clear when Carrie Leljedal, the mother of 25-year-old Sturge-Weber Syndrome patient Lynn Ray, contacted Ida. Carrie and her son Lynn have been following my journey and asked if I could come to St. Louis, Missouri to meet them and visit St. Louis Children's Hospital where Lynn receives treatment. Not long after, Ida spoke with Kristy McGrady, the mother of 11-year-old Sturge-Weber Syndrome patient Paige. They too live near St. Louis Children's Hospital and would like to meet me. Needless to say, there was no need for further discussion on which route I should take. I am going to St. Louis to meet Lynn and Paige, and I am excited and honored to do it.

In order to get to St. Louis from Tucumcari, I needed to start going in a northeasterly direction, so in the morning I bid I-40 a fond farewell. Despite my two flat tires outside of Kingman, Arizona, it treated me well. I then stopped at a convenience store near my motel for Clif Bars (my go-to source of nourishment on the road) and directions to Highway 54 (the road Ida had instructed me to follow). There, a cashier named Emma pointed me in the right direction and wished me good luck. It was a nice start to the day and to the next leg of my journey.

I soon learned that Highway 54 isn't much of a highway at all. It's one lane running each way through open fields and farmland. With the exception of the occasional passing vehicle, it seemed deserted and reminded me of the desolate stretch of Route 66 I encountered on my way to Barstow, California. Even the one proper town I passed through appeared lifeless, a ghost town in a forgotten land.

View from Hwy 54 near Dalhart, TX.

In the late morning, I came upon a camper on the side of the road. In it were traveling retirees Ted and Liz from Charlton, Massachusetts. I was excited to see them – actually, I would have been excited to see *anyone* at that point – so I stopped to say hello. After introducing myself and telling them about Jenna and our cause, Ted told me about his brother-in-law who is extremely ill with Mantle Cell Lymphoma. Sad to say, it seems the hardships of illness affect us all.

That afternoon, I came to the New Mexico/Texas state line. It's always fun crossing from one state into the next. However, the "Welcome to Texas" sign made it more funny than fun. The sign couldn't have been more than half the size of the Arizona and New Mexico signs I'd seen. And to think, they say everything is bigger in Texas. Well, apparently not everything.

Al DeCesaris in front of the Texas sign on Hwy 54 near Dalhart, TX.

# Day 17 (9/24/13): Dalhart, TX to Liberal, KS [112 miles]

The plan for the day was to ride 100+ miles from Texas to Oklahoma and eventually into Kansas. It seemed ambitious, but the terrain was flat, the weather was nice, and I was feeling good. "Make hay," my older brother Joe had told me, referring to the expression "make hay while the sun shines." And that's exactly what I intended to do.

Although Highway 54 through the Texas panhandle is flat, it does present its share of challenges. For one thing, it seems to be the habitat of every type of flying insect in the world (a few of which I think I inadvertently ingested). No offense to any Texans out there, but it is by far the most uninspiring scenery I've ever seen. Even the Mojave Desert has more charm to it. Well, maybe that's an overstatement, but make no mistake, farm after farm after farm can get painfully monotonous. And the smells … oh, the smells! If I learn nothing else from this stretch of Highway 54, I now know that cattle trucks, which seem to roll incessantly through these parts, give off one horrendous stench.

After I had come to terms with flying nuisances, humdrum scenery, and nauseating smells, I stopped on the side of the road to have lunch. Unfortunately, before

I had even taken the first bite of my White Chocolate Macadamia Nut Clif Bar – you would think I have a controlling interest in the Clif Bar company as much money as I've shelled out to them – it slipped out of my hand and fell to the ground. Now, before you read the rest of this and shudder in disgust, know that I need to eat an absurd amount of food each day to sustain my energy, and that I don't have an unlimited supply of food on my bike. Anyway, I scooped up the Clif Bar, brushed it off, and gave it a quick once-over before wolfing it down ... all the while hoping the "Five-Second" rule applies out on the open road.

In the early afternoon, I made my first crossing of the day and entered Oklahoma. Believe it or not, the sign welcoming travelers to "The Sooner State" was even more laughable than the one welcoming people to "The Lone Star State." It was ridiculously small and had the look of a bad arts-and-crafts project.

Al DeCesaris in front of the Oklahoma sign on Hwy 54 near Texhoma, OK.

That evening, however, my faith in the Great Plains States was restored when I approached the Kansas state line and saw their professionally designed welcome sign.

Al DeCesaris in front of the Kansas sign on Hwy 54 near Liberal, KS.

As I entered the town of Liberal and approached my motel, I reflected on how I had ridden through three states and covered 112 miles during the course of the day – my biggest day yet. Still, the day was not over.

Just a few blocks from the motel, I saw a sign for *Dorothy's House* and was reminded of something Jenna had recently said to me, "Follow the yellow brick road." I'm not sure why she said that, maybe she had recently seen the movie, *The Wizard of Oz*, but her words resonated with me. Even though the sun was low in the sky and I was dog-tired, I rode over to *Dorothy's House* to have a look. To my surprise, there in the heart of Liberal, Kansas was a replica of Dorothy's house from

*The Wizard of Oz.* Also, on the grounds near the house was a statue of Dorothy with Toto in her arms and images of the Scarecrow, Tin Man, and Cowardly Lion. And sure enough, leading to the promise of better days, was the yellow brick road Jenna had told me to follow.

Novara Randonee at *Dorothy's House & Land of Oz* in Liberal, KS.

# Day 18 (9/25/13): Liberal, KS to Greensburg, KS [102 miles]

A couple of hours into the day's ride, I saw a man on the opposite side of Highway 54 pedaling toward me. He appeared to have a bike similar to mine with jam-packed panniers hanging from his bike rack and a tent and sleeping bag secured atop it. I knew this wasn't someone just cruising around. We both came to a stop, and the man introduced himself as Bud Greeley from Bluffton, Minnesota. I was astonished to learn that this 67-year-old was biking from Bluffton all the way to Fountain Hills, Arizona (over 1,800 miles) in honor of his great niece Phoebe to create awareness and raise funds for the National Down Syndrome Society.

Bud and I discussed our causes, shared riding tips, and had an uplifting and encouraging conversation. When the time came to continue on, we wished each other well and set out on our individual paths. It was a real pleasure to meet Bud and to learn about Phoebe. I hope he has a safe ride and raises much awareness and lots of money for his cause.

"May the wind be always at your back" is a line from an Irish blessing I've been hearing quite a bit these days. Although I didn't fully grasp its significance (that was until I started biking through Kansas), I did appreciate people saying it to me. And I will appreciate it even more in the future because, for the first few hours of the day I had a strong Kansas wind at my back and in the afternoon that same strong Kansas wind was hitting me from the side, making things onerous. At one point the gusts grew so strong that dust from nearby fields started flying through the air, forcing me to take the Buff (the "multi-tasking bandana" or so its website boasts) I wore on my head and put it over my mouth and nose like an Old West cowboy. I must admit, I thought it was kind of cool at first, but the novelty of it soon wore off, and my progress, as you would expect, was dreadfully slow.

Al DeCesaris on Hwy 54 near Plains, KS.

Later in the day, I stopped at a convenience store for Gatorade and Clif Bars (if you're tired of hearing about Clif Bars, just think how tired I am of eating them). The salesclerk was a friendly South African guy named

Johann (or so I thought; with that accent of his I wasn't exactly sure what he said). When he heard where my journey had started, his eyes lit up with excitement. Sometimes I need to see the reaction of others to realize just how far I've come.

The rest of the day proved equally challenging with the wind gusting to over 20 mph. It seems in Kansas the wind can be your best friend or your worst enemy. Today, it was both, for in the morning I was pedaling along without a care in the world and just a few hours later I was fighting for every last inch. This very well may have been one of the hardest days I've endured on the road thus far, but somehow, by day's end, I had another century ride to my credit and managed to make it safely to my destination of Greensburg.

Before I set out on this journey, I never imagined I'd be biking 100 miles in a day (and multiple times, no less), but damn if I'm not doing it. Without a doubt, the prayers, support, and encouragement of family, friends, and even perfect strangers (like the salesclerk at the convenience store) have helped immensely. And Irish blessings don't hurt either, especially when you're biking through the wind tunnel that is Kansas.

# Day 19 (9/26/13): Greensburg, KS to Cheney, KS [80 miles]

For the second day in a row I had to battle strong wind, which again hampered my progress and frustrated me to no end. It was like trudging uphill in deep snow – difficult, slow going, and exhausting. Even the declines didn't provide relief because I was forced to ride the brakes and clench the handlebars for fear of being blown over. Within a few hours, my legs had grown weary, my hands sore, and my spirits dejected.

View from Hwy 54 near Greensburg, KS.

In the afternoon, I stopped on the side of the road to have a bite to eat and regroup. As I did, a man named Doug Myers pulled over to see if I was okay. With a mouth full of some chocolaty protein bar (which probably made me look like I was missing teeth), I assured him that I was all right and then took the opportunity to tell him about *Crossing America For A Cure*.

Doug listened with keen interest and offered encouragement. He then told me that he was preparing for a charity bike ride of his own in memory of his 5-year-old daughter Annie, whom he lost last year to an immune disorder called Hemophagocytic Lymphohistiocytosis (HLH). I was stunned by what he told me and terribly saddened at the realization that this man, who had pulled over to see if I was okay, was going through one of the worst possible experiences a parent could endure. Yet, as awful as the news was to hear, Doug's will and determination, as well as his love for his daughter Annie and his wife and son, were both hopeful and inspiring. I pray Doug's ride will bring attention to HLH and bring his family comfort and peace. From that moment on, I stopped complaining about the wind, my fatigue and soreness, and just rode.

My plan for the day was to make it to Goddard, where I would meet Cheryl and Travis Brock (friends of my sister) and ride back with them to their house for the night. However, as the day drew on, I knew I wasn't going to make it all the way to Goddard; there were still many miles to cover and little time. So, after discussing the situation with the Brocks, Travis drove out to where I was (some 45 minutes from his house) to pick me up. For those keeping track at home, Travis picked me up on Highway 54 at mile marker 187. So when I set out again tomorrow, that's where I'll begin my ride.

Once the bike was loaded into the bed of Travis' truck, we headed east toward his house. Along the way we stopped at a local bike shop called the Bicycle

Pedaler. There, a knowledgeable young man named Quentin tightened the gear shifter (it had become loose), and checked the chain and tire pressure. While he serviced the bike, the owner of the shop, Ruth, set me up with supplies and mapped out a route around Wichita and into Missouri. The service they provided was excellent.

Soon after, we arrived at the Brock home and I met Travis' warmhearted wife Cheryl and their children Hannah, Leah, and Luke. Everyone was so hospitable and made me feel right at home. I was also treated to have a fantastic home-cooked meal. Travis' parents are cattle ranchers, and the rib-eye steaks they served were "Brock beef." These steaks would give even the finest steakhouses a run for their money. And Cheryl's homemade apple pie was, without a doubt, one of the best I've ever had. In a day when I was reminded of the importance of family, I was grateful to be able to spend the evening with such a loving and caring one.

# Day 20 (9/27/13): Cheney, KS to Eureka, KS [96 miles]

After another delicious home-cooked meal and a little more quality-time with the Brock family, I said my goodbyes to Cheryl and the kids, and Travis drove me back to mile marker 187 (yesterday's ending point). You may think making Travis drive 45 minutes west of his house to bring me back to the exact spot he picked me up at is a bit over-the-top, especially since I'd be biking along that same stretch of road as I made my way east. But, if I'm going to bike 3,000+ miles across the entire U.S., I want to pedal through each and every mile I can.

As soon as I started out, I realized it was going to be another difficult day battling the wind. Prior to setting out on this journey, I had been told (numerous times) that Kansas is *always* windy. I figured people were just exaggerating. Well, apparently they weren't. To add to my troubles, my hands were bothering me again and my hip had started to hurt. I knew the soreness in my hands was the result of gripping the handlebars too tightly (which is hard not to do when the wind is constantly pushing you around), but the discomfort in my hip had me confused and concerned.

As though on cue, I received a call from Bryan Springer (between him, John Wall, and John Gallagher,

I have an A+ medical team looking out for me). After explaining to him what I was feeling, Bryan diagnosed what was causing my hip discomfort and recommended ways to treat it. I've already forgotten the medical term he used to describe the problem, but the bottom line is 20 straight days on a bicycle comes with its fair share of pain and discomfort. It's pretty much unavoidable.

Not long after talking with my old friend and receiving much-needed medical advice, iTunes shuffled to the song, "With a little help from my friends." As I listened to McCartney and Lennon's lyrics, I realized that, like the song says, I am getting by with a little help from my friends – actually, with a *lot of help* from my friends. In fact, what I'm doing, what *we all* are doing, for those suffering with Sturge-Weber Syndrome would not be possible without the help of friends new and old.

View from Hwy 54 near Rosalia, KS.

Toward the end of the day, my brother Joe called to pass along some great news. The Greene Turtle Sports

Bar & Grille has agreed to join us in the fight against Sturge-Weber Syndrome by becoming a *Crossing America For A Cure* event sponsor. As part of their contribution to the cause, they'll host a celebration when I come through Maryland at their Annapolis location. As for the exact date and time of the event, we're not quite sure yet ... it all depends on how fast I can pedal.

After a long, hard day of riding past prairies and farmland – lots and lots of farmland – I arrived at the Blue Stem Lodge in Eureka. And not a minute too soon because, by the time I checked into my room (dragging my tried-and-true Novara Randonee bicycle in with me), the sky had grown dark.

Although my days are rarely predictable, my nights usually follow the same routine. This one began as most do, with an "I made it safely" phone call to my family, a hot shower (which included the hand-washing of my cycling outfit), and the ordering of a large cheese pizza with grilled chicken. And, yes, I ate the whole thing myself ... crust and all.

# Day 21 (9/28/13): Eureka, KS to Iola, KS [51 miles]

In sports, they call it a rain delay. I'll call it a reprieve. It was the first day of pouring rain since I started my journey, though I wasn't complaining. After 20 straight days on the road, my body needed a break and the extra sleep was much appreciated.

It was close to noon when the rain let up. With a bit of disappointment – I was *really* hoping it would rain all day – I re-packed my panniers. I inevitably end up emptying them each night in search of something or the other that fell to the bottom. I then donned my cycling outfit (the dry set, of course, because the one I wore yesterday was still damp from last night's washing) and got myself prepared, mentally and physically, to hit the road.

Leaving the warm, dry motel room, I returned to the lonely farm-lined road en route to the city of Iola. Although the rest of the day was dry, the sun remained hidden, making for a dreary ride.

Not far down the road, I heard dogs barking and turned to see two German Shepherds racing across a fenced-in yard. I had seen this plenty of times before so I paid it little regard. However, when I looked back, I saw that the dogs had somehow gotten out of the yard and were charging toward me. Before I knew it, the larger of the two (of course, it had to be the larger one) was closing in on me, and fast. I pedaled as hard as I could, but wasn't able to outrun him. Just as the lead dog bared his large, jagged teeth (and sized up my right leg for his afternoon snack), I screamed "Nooooo!" at the top of my lungs. It seemed to startle the dogs, but it took a second guttural scream and some Lance Armstrong-like pedaling to make the dogs abandon their pursuit. I don't want to say I was scared (and I definitely don't want to put that in writing), so let's just say I was *somewhat* concerned.

About an hour later, I came across a rest area. Although I didn't have to stop at that time, I figured I'd use the restroom since it was right there. Yet, as luck would have it, when I stepped to the urinal my cell phone somehow slipped out of my jacket pocket and fell right in (yep ... right ... in ... the urinal). The sight of my phone sitting at the bottom of the *freshly-scrubbed and hygienically-cleaned* urinal – don't laugh, I *have to believe* that – was even more frightening than the bloodthirsty dogs trying to sink their teeth into me. Needless to say, I spent the next 30 minutes washing and disinfecting every nook and cranny of my phone.

In the late afternoon, Ida started calling motels in Iola to try to find a room for me. We usually wait until about 3:00 pm before securing a place to stay since it's hard to determine how many miles I'll cover on a given day. However, on this day, we waited too long. By the time the calls were made, all of the motels in the area were booked solid. Apparently, there's a Buster Keaton festival in Iola this weekend (for those who don't know, Keaton was a Kansas-born actor/writer/filmmaker best known for his silent films.), and large crowds were pouring into the city for the festivities. I know, I find it hard to believe myself.

Ida did have better luck with a local church. An elderly couple from their congregation offered to let me stay at their home for the night. It was a very kind offer, but the couple lived a good distance from the city, which would have meant another hour or so in the saddle. In the end, one of the motels Ida called had a cancellation and was able to get me in. Before going to the motel, I stopped at a convenience store for drinks and snacks. While I was there, the elderly couple from the church pulled into the parking lot. It seems they'd been driving around Iola looking for me to make sure I was okay. It was yet another example of how caring and supportive the people I've met on this journey have been.

View from Hwy 54 near Yates Center, KS.

## Day 22 (9/29/13): Iola, KS to Weaubleau, MO [106 miles]

For the first time, in what felt like a very long time, there were no troublesome winds slowing me down. And the repetitive flat terrain with its fields of wheat, corn, and grain had started to give way to rolling hills and lush meadows. It was as though I was again leaving one distinct land and entering another. And sure enough, in the midst of this transition, I came upon a sign welcoming travelers to "The Show Me State."

View from Hwy 54 near Bronson, KS.

Missouri is the seventh state I've biked in since I began *Crossing America For A Cure*, and represents a remarkable accomplishment, for I'm now more than halfway through my cross-country bicycle journey. My excitement must have been evident because a young woman went out of her way to stop and take a photo of me in front of the sign. It was great to get a picture in front of a state sign that wasn't a selfie for once. A few awkward dance moves ensued. Like I said, I was excited.

Al DeCesaris in front of the Missouri sign on Hwy 54 near Deerfield, MO.

I then called Ida to give her an update on my location and share the good news. She was almost as excited as I was. However, the tone of the conversation quickly changed when she informed me that there were no accommodations to be found before the city of Weaubleau, which was 100+ miles from my starting point and still another 60 miles down the road. That presented a major problem because, based on the number of miles I average per hour and the number of hours of daylight then remaining, I'd be on the road well after sundown. At the realization of that, the panic light in the back of my head started to flash, and with it began another stressful race against the setting sun.

Highway 54 through these parts seemed to have more ups and downs than a roller coaster. Unlike my rides in Kansas, where insufferable wind forced me to take declines (the few I encountered) at a snail's pace, here I was able to use the declines to my advantage by shifting into higher gears and pedaling hard as I descended. This allowed me to gain a tremendous amount of speed on the backside of hills, which in turn helped me quickly climb the hills that followed. Over the next several hours I rode tirelessly, making the most of each pedal stroke, and reached Weaubleau just before the sun dipped below the horizon.

As I entered the city – with a population of just over 400, it isn't much of a city at all – I was feeling quite proud of what I had just achieved and for logging another century ride. Before heading to my motel, I rode to a convenience store to grab something to eat and coasted into the parking lot with a satisfied grin on my face. Yet, as I brought my bike to a stop, I unclipped my left foot from the pedal and mistakenly leaned to the right. It was a costly error that sent me (and my bike) crashing onto the pavement.

The humbling and jarring experience brought a biblical passage to mind – "Pride goeth before destruction, and a haughty spirit before a fall." As I warily pedaled to the tiny cabin where I'm staying for the night, and the pain of *my fall* began to set in, I started to think that the old passage might indeed have some truth to it.

# Day 23 (9/30/13): Weaubleau, MO to St. Robert, MO [93 miles]

It only took a few miles of riding for me to realize that my bike wasn't 100 percent. Last night's fall had left the gears out of whack ... as it had left me. My right forearm and elbow hurt, and my lower back and wrists bothered me as well.

Not much farther down the road, I came across an older gentleman named Gary who was out enjoying a morning bike ride. He stopped to say hello, and I soon learned that he's a member of a local cycling club. When I told him what I was doing, he couldn't have been more excited. Bicycling across the country is something he has wanted to do since he was a kid. I guess you can say it's on his "bucket list." It's funny how things work out because it was never on mine. And, until recently, it wasn't something I ever imagined doing.

In the early afternoon, I left Highway 54 at Camdenton and picked up Route 7, which appeared to be the quickest and easiest way to get to Interstate 44 and, ultimately, to St. Louis. Yet, after a few miles, the straight, wide-shouldered highway became a winding country road with no shoulder at all. Even worse, there were rumble strips (the deepest ones I'd seen) running through the white lines on both sides of the road.

This was one of the most dangerous roads, if not *the most dangerous road*, I had been on thus far. Whenever I heard a car coming up behind me, I moved over to the right as far as I could and prayed the driver saw me. It was nerve-racking to say the least.

At some point, I heard an SUV barreling up behind me and hastily moved to the far right side of the lane to get out of its way. However, when I did, I went over too far and caught my front tire on the rumble strip and lost control of the bike. Within seconds, I was off the road and my front tire jackknifed, sending me flying over the handlebars. My left forearm took the brunt of the fall and I ended up sprawled out in the grass on the side of the road. The crash left my body battered and bruised and my forearm a bloody mess. As for my bike, with the exception of the chain falling off and a few scuffs, it was fine. (And that, my friends, is why I'm riding this ridiculously heavy steel-frame bike.)

After a phone call to my sister for some much-needed consoling, I cleaned my arm, fixed the chain, and continued on (albeit gingerly). By the time I reached I-44, the sun was down and my motel was still a ways off. So, I attached my bike light to the handlebars and pedaled off into the dark for the first (and hopefully last) time. Although riding at night isn't something I plan to make a habit of, it wasn't as bad as I thought it'd be. Of course, it helped having Ida on the phone directing me and keeping me calm. And surprisingly, the gear problem I noticed earlier no longer seemed to be an issue. Who knows, maybe the crash put things back in whack. An hour or so later, I exited I-44 and hopped onto Route 66, where my motel was located. No, that's not a typo. I was back on the famous old road yet again.

Once I got to my room, I called Bryan Springer to let him know about the crash and all of my aches and pains. His primary concern was whether I'd suffered a head injury. After a battery of questions, he determined that my brain was still working as well (or as badly) as it always had. Although, as a precautionary measure, he suggested I arrange a middle of the night wake-up call. If I answered, I was good to go. If I didn't ... well, Bryan didn't exactly tell me what that would have meant. Thankfully, I answered the phone when it rang. Although it was after several nervous attempts to reach me and just minutes before a 911 call, or so I was later told. Just the same, when Day 23 was done, I was concussion-free and my bike was working better than ever.

The Gasconade River from Rt 7 near Richland, MO.

# Day 24 (10/1/13): St. Robert, MO to Gray Summit, MO [94 miles]

The first day of October proved to be a great day. Actually, just getting out of bed without any pain after yesterday's wreck would have made it a great day. Yet, it was more than that. Plans were finalized for tomorrow's visit with Lynn Ray and Paige McGrady and the day's 90+ mile ride on Interstate 44 went like clockwork – no flat tires, no falls and, most important, no crashes.

After the debacle that was yesterday, I received numerous phone calls from my family to see how I was feeling. It was nice to hear from everyone and know how concerned they were for my safety. It was par for the course though – between my parents and three siblings, not more than a few hours ever go by without someone calling to check in on me – the damn phone is constantly ringing. All kidding aside, their love, support, and encouragement have been truly amazing.

Around 11:00 am, I came across an overpass and stopped underneath it to take a break in the shade. Even though the sweltering desert heat is well behind me, the security and shelter of an overpass still has its benefits. And this particular one had a low rock wall under it with a recess, which made for a recliner of sorts where I could kick back and enjoy a little R&R.

Al DeCesaris under an overpass on I-44 near Rolla, MO.

In the early afternoon, I stopped at a convenience store and met a guy named Hal who was on his way to Austin, Texas. With a thick southern accent, he asked where I was biking to. When I told Hal where I was headed, he couldn't believe it. It wasn't true disbelief, mind you; it was more like amazement. He snapped a picture of me to show his friends in Texas the "bicycle dude," as he referred to me. As I pedaled off, I wondered if I will have that same sense of amazement when I look back on this journey when all is said and done.

Later in the day, I spoke to one of my best friends from college, Mike Cannone. We had been playing phone tag since I left California, and it was great to finally catch up. We talked for some time about the crazy adventures I've been having and about all the wonderful people I've met along the way. At the end of our conversation, his 2½-year-old son Cody got on the phone and yelled, "Go, Al!" His enthusiasm was contagious and brought a big smile to my face.

My one gripe for the day (no day is complete without at least one) was the number of armadillos I saw on the road. I seriously think I came across two dozen of them. They're the strangest looking creatures (especially when flattened by an eighteen-wheeler) and don't smell particularly pleasant either. I guess they're better than tarantulas and snakes though. Since the journey began, I've seen three of the hairy eight-legged spiders (as you're well aware from my whining) and a couple of snakes slithering across my path. Other than angry canines, I can't think of anything that could get me pedaling faster. Still, the strange and smelly armadillo isn't an animal I hope to see again anytime soon.

View from I-44 near Villa Ridge, MO.

In the late afternoon, I came to an area where I-44 shot between fragmented rock walls topped with dense woodland. Although there were a few tough climbs, the unique terrain made for an enjoyable ride. And it was cool to see hints of orange (the first signs of autumn) in the leaves on the trees. As I've made my way across the country, I've seen the scenery change time and again. Now it seems I'll be witness to the change of seasons.

My day of riding ended at a gas station in Gray Summit where I met Ken Stark, the father of my good friend Michelle (better known as Mishi). As Mishi had kindly arranged, her parents are hosting me in their home for two nights while I'm in the area (and, of course, going to bring me back to that same gas station in Gray Summit when I resume my journey).

Once my bike and gear were loaded up in Ken's vehicle, he drove us to his house where his lovely wife Ginny was busy preparing dinner for us. After getting cleaned up, I enjoyed a wonderful meal and a relaxing evening with the Starks and their adorable King Charles Spaniel, Pocket. Like I said, it was a great day, and tomorrow promises to be a great one as well.

# Day 25 (10/2/13): St. Louis, MO

As I look back on the first few weeks of this journey, I realize that our focus was a bit narrow as we put almost all of our efforts into creating awareness and raising funds for research (and pedaling, of course). Although creating awareness and raising funds are extremely important and will continue to be our primary focus, *Crossing America For A Cure* is also about giving hope to those suffering with Sturge-Weber Syndrome and inspiring others to join the fight against this devastating neurological disorder. When the parents of Lynn Ray and Paige McGrady let Ida know that their children wanted to meet me, I was reminded of that fact. And seeing that Lynn and Paige (along with Jenna and all the other Sturge-Weber Syndrome patients) are the very reason I'm biking across America, having the chance to meet them and let them know that there are people fighting for them was an opportunity I wasn't going to pass up.

The minute I saw Lynn and Paige and their families, and saw the smiles on their faces, I recognized just how far-reaching this charitable event has become. And as I shook Lynn's hand and hugged Paige, and felt their appreciation for what we (all of us) are doing for them, I became aware of the positive effects our efforts are having on their lives. The realization of it all was both eye-opening and inspiring.

Paige McGrady, Al DeCesaris, Lynn Ray at St. Louis Children's Hospital in St. Louis, MO
(photo courtesy of Kristy McGrady).

Lynn's mom Carrie gave me a heartfelt hug and some trail mix for the road. Paige and her parents, Wade and Kristy, gave me a gift bag with energy bars, a cool St. Louis Cardinals t-shirt, and a Rainbow Loom bracelet for Jenna. If nothing else makes it to Maryland, that bracelet most definitely will. In addition, Paige made an amazing sign that read, "THANK YOU, AL! Keep pedaling! You can do it! ♥ Paige McGrady."

We spent the next several hours together touring St. Louis Children's Hospital where Lynn and Paige receive treatment. During that time, I learned a great deal about both of them, the difficulties they face, their daily struggles, as well as their likes and interests. It was an unbelievable experience, far greater than I ever could have imagined. Even though this day didn't involve any biking (which, by the way, I'm really starting to enjoy), it has been the highlight of my journey.

That evening Ginny and Ken Stark took me to a local restaurant where we met their son Chris and his wife Melissa. The food was great and the company was even better. The evening was carefree and fun, but when the conversation shifted to my day with Lynn and Paige, I couldn't help but get a little emotional.

Although our time together was brief, Lynn and Paige left an indelible mark on me. Like Jenna, they fight this devastating disorder each and every day, which is something most of us (including myself) will never *truly* understand. Yet, I do know enough about Sturge-Weber Syndrome to know that they need our help.

Even though I'm just an ordinary man, I have belief and determination, and I will continue to fight for all those suffering with Sturge-Weber Syndrome – be it with my legs, my mind, my voice. And I hope others will too. For in each of us is the power to make a difference!

# Day 26 (10/3/13): Gray Summit, MO to Collinsville, IL [60 miles]

Today I rode in honor of Lynn Ray, the young man I had the privilege of meeting yesterday at St. Louis Children's Hospital. Although the day had its share of adversity (as most do), it ended in the fine company of Lynn's mother Carrie and her husband Jason, and was by and large a success.

After I said goodbye to Ken Stark and thanked him and his wife Ginny for their hospitality, Ginny drove me to the gas station in Gray Summit where I last left off. From there I took Route 100 East (aka Historic U.S. 66) for about 20 miles. I then followed Clayton Road into the western portion of St. Louis, passing through several upscale areas before reaching Forest Park.

Known as the "heart of St. Louis," Forest Park is a 1,371-acre public park, which was home to the 1904 Summer Olympics and is currently home to the Saint Louis Zoo, the Saint Louis Art Museum, the Missouri History Museum, and the Saint Louis Science Center. In the park I saw a U.S. Navy "Blue Angels" fighter jet, a Triceratops, and its nemesis the Tyrannosaurus Rex ... and I have photos to prove it. It was great to take a leisurely ride on a bike path through a park as opposed to dodging cars and trucks on a busy road.

Not far from the park I came across notable landmarks such as the Cathedral Basilica of Saint Louis, Saint Louis University, and the Fox Theatre, before coming to a neglected part of the city near the McKinley Bridge. I was advised to take that bridge because it has a separate area for pedestrians and cyclists. The problem was, after getting turned around and riding past the bridge a handful of times, frustrations were high and I mistakenly took the wrong ramp onto the bridge and ended up on the section designated for vehicular traffic. This wasn't a minor slip-up, mind you. This was a major mistake, and it nearly got me creamed by an eighteen-wheeler. I think my life tried to flash before my eyes, but I was pedaling too fast to notice.

After some pressure-packed pedaling and prayers to the Man Upstairs, I found an opening where I was able to cross over to the pedestrian/cyclist area and slid between the barriers to safety. It was one of the most dangerous situations I've been in thus far (and that's saying something because I've been in several extremely precarious ones). After breathing a huge sigh of relief, I snapped photos of the Illinois State sign (which stood at the middle of the bridge), the Mississippi River, and the St. Louis skyline with its famous Gateway Arch. I then got back on my bike and coasted across the rest of the bridge into Illinois.

I continued on for another couple of hours before reaching Collinsville where I had planned to pick up the interstate. However, to my disappointment, I discovered (by way of a sign at the on-ramp) that use of the interstate by non-motorized traffic is prohibited. The lawyer in me had me thinking that I could win the argument that the sign didn't actually restrict bicycles ... the language was *somewhat* ambiguous. Lawyer logic aside, the sun had begun its descent and, not knowing which route I should take, it seemed best to call it a day.

After reaching out to Carrie and Jason to let them know where I was, Jason came and picked me up and brought me back to their home. That evening I enjoyed a tasty pot roast dinner and meaningful conversation and got to learn more about Lynn and his struggles living with Sturge-Weber Syndrome.

Like I said before, it wasn't the smoothest of days, but when it was done I had navigated the "Gateway to the West," crossed the "Mighty Mississippi," entered the "Land of Lincoln" (my 8th state), and spent a wonderful evening in the company of Lynn's loving family on the very day I rode in honor of that inspiring young man.

Al DeCesaris in front of the Illinois sign on the McKinley Bridge in St. Louis, MO.

# Day 27 (10/4/13): Collinsville, IL to Salem, IL [68 miles]

You would think after the wonderful evening I had yesterday with Carrie and Jason, and the amazing day I had on Wednesday at St. Louis Children's Hospital, that I'd be recharged and raring to go. Oddly, that wasn't the case. In fact, it was quite the opposite.

In the morning, Carrie dropped me off in Collinsville at the spot where I left off yesterday. After saying our goodbyes, I started out along a route that Jason had been good enough to map out for me. (This route had me taking Route 40 since, as I learned yesterday, bicycling on interstates is prohibited in Illinois.) However, after discussing the plan with Ida, I started to wonder if this was the best way for me to go. Jason had mapped out the route based on the premise that I wanted to head toward Indianapolis. Yet, as Ida informed me, Indy was only on our radar because the interstate heading in that direction was relatively straight and flat; it seemed as though it would be a much easier ride than the other easterly roads. But since I couldn't ride on the interstate anyway, there was no reason to go in that direction. She also pointed out that the majority of the eastern states prohibit bicycle riding on interstates, which only helped to complicate matters.

Although I knew she was probably right, no longer having a definitive plan and not knowing which route to take left me frustrated. Not to mention, I'd gotten comfortable riding on interstates and the thought of having to bike on smaller roads with limited shoulders, like the one I crashed on, had me worried. As Ida researched our options, I stood on the side of the road wondering if the route we decided on would get me safely to my next destination or just cause me more problems. For the first time in a long time, doubt started to take hold and my confidence wavered. Even though I'd already faced a number of difficult challenges, this uncertainty and self-doubt were *extremely* hard to deal with. I now know what people mean when they say an endeavor like this is more challenging mentally than it is physically.

While I waited to hear back from Ida, I put a call in to my dad to get his thoughts on the matter. Just as he has time and again throughout this journey (and throughout my life), he offered words of encouragement and the kind of support only a father can give. Soon after, Ida called and told me she had determined that taking Route 50 toward Cincinnati was my best option. Although I had my reservations, I followed her recommendation and headed back to Collinsville to get to Route 50.

I hated having to backtrack, but it felt good to be moving again and to have a plan in place. Plus, it afforded me the opportunity to ride past the world's largest catsup bottle (a 170-foot-tall water tower reproduction of a Brooks Old Original Catsup bottle) which, believe it or not, is a famous local attraction. And to think, I'd thought the Buster Keaton festival was strange. This wacky slice of Americana makes that seem perfectly normal.

To my relief, Route 50 was in good repair and, for the most part, had a manageable shoulder. It took me through quaint rural communities and picturesque farmland. Still, I didn't feel great about things, and couldn't seem to shake the doubt I was feeling.

View from Rt 50 near Trenton, IL.

Not long after, Ida called and read to me a letter Kristy McGrady (Paige's mom) had written about my efforts and our recent meeting at the hospital.

"Al is biking across America to raise awareness and funds for Sturge-Weber Syndrome. As most of you know, this is the medical condition that Paige was diagnosed with 5 years ago. SWS is very rare and there are few chances for us to connect with people in the area that have it. So, you can imagine our excitement at the opportunity to meet someone who is pedaling over 3,000 miles to raise awareness!!!"

"We spent a couple of hours on Wednesday, October 3 with Al and a young man from Illinois who also has SWS. Al shared several heart-warming stories about his journey with us. ... Al chatted with Paige and took the time to learn more about her experience with SWS. We also heard about Al's family ... particularly his niece, Jenna, for whom he is riding. He is one proud uncle!!! There are truly not enough adjectives to describe this man ... kind, humble, generous, selfless, strong, brave. You get the idea! :-)

"Our time with Al inspired us to do something that is a bit out of character for us. ... With that being said, we decided to open a "Street Page" in Paige's name...."

Kristy's heartfelt words, and her and her husband Wade's desire to join us in raising funds for the cause (through the fundraising team they set up on the *Crossing America For A Cure* website) reaffirmed the importance of what I was doing and reminded me of the significance of today's ride. For today I rode in honor of Paige (my plan is to dedicate a day's ride to each of the Sturge-Weber patients who are following my journey) and thoughts of that brave little girl and her loving parents helped motivate me and put my doubts to rest.

It's funny; as difficult as the day was (maybe one of the most difficult), it was also one of the most rewarding. It showed me that, with support and encouragement, adversity can be overcome.

# Day 28 (10/5/13): Salem, IL

Rain equals rest for me, and since the day brought heavy rains, I did a lot of resting. However, as much as I enjoyed sleeping in and giving my weary body a break, it did get boring. You think being stuck at home on a rainy day is tough; try being in a roadside motel by yourself in the middle of nowhere. That'll give you some serious cabin fever ... trust me!

Yet, a day like this also lends itself to self-reflection (not that 8 to 10 hours a day on a bike doesn't) and can help one see things more clearly (like the rationale behind a 3,000+ mile bicycle ride). As you can imagine, people keep asking what made me decide to bike across America. And often times the question is followed by a reference to *Forrest Gump* or, even better, a quote from the movie. Although I love that movie, and have a good laugh every time someone repeats one of Forrest's iconic lines (and there are plenty of them), I didn't embark on this journey because "I just felt like running." And not because *I just felt like biking* either. Sitting on a leather bike saddle all day long isn't exactly my idea of a good time.

This endeavor wasn't taken on capriciously either. A lot of careful planning and preparation went into it. My mom and younger brother Michael – both of whom put in countless hours of painstaking work before I even logged my first mile – can attest to that. And, most important, it has a purpose, a true and worthwhile purpose.

Still, when I made the decision to do this, I had no idea what my efforts would actually bring. Would our message be heard? Would people support the cause? Would I be able to bike the entire way? There were questions, doubts, and naysayers (as there always are). In a lot of ways, I liken my decision to take on this journey more to what transpired in the movie *Field of Dreams* (if we're going to stick to movie references, that is).

In that movie (and if you've never seen it, you really need to), the main character played by Kevin Costner hears a voice in his cornfield that says, "If you build it, he will come," and has a vision of a baseball diamond, which inspires him to plow under his corn and build a baseball field. He has no idea what his efforts will bring, but he takes a leap of faith because he feels it is something he needs to do, something he was called to do. Now I never heard voices in a cornfield (at least not until I rode through Kansas), but, like Costner's character, I believe this is something I was meant to do.

Although my family and I have hosted other charitable events, we had never done anything like this. Even more surprising, I hadn't ridden a bicycle more than 10 miles in a day (if that) until a few weeks before the journey began. Despite all of that, I chose to take on this 3,000+ mile endeavor for Jenna and all those suffering with Sturge-Weber Syndrome, to give them hope, to inspire others to get involved, to create awareness, and to raise funds to further the efforts to find a cure. And, by the grace of God, we're making it happen, one mile at a time.

Jenna Heck (photo courtesy of Ida Heck).

# Day 29 (10/6/13): Salem, IL to Bedford, IL [148 miles]

I woke to great weather and set out on Route 50 toward the rising sun with the wind at my back. After yesterday's heavy rains, it was nice to see the sun shining again and even better to have the wind helping me along.

Not far into my ride, I saw a runner coming toward me. He must have seen the big red, white, and blue *Crossing America For A Cure* logo on my cycling jersey and realized I was doing a charity ride because he started clapping as I approached him. When we passed each other, he asked where I had started and where I was headed. "West Coast to East Coast," I told him. The man responded with a big smile and loud cheers. His enthusiasm for what I was doing made my morning.

Whether it was the rest I had gotten yesterday, the wind aiding me, or the flat terrain (probably a bit of all three), I made great time. Actually, I made phenomenal time and would have made even better time had I not had to get off of Route 50 when I did (there was a 10+ mile stretch that prohibited bicycles).

On the alternate route, I came across the Lincoln Trail State Memorial, a sculpture commemorating Abraham Lincoln's first entrance into Illinois.

Novara Randonee at the Lincoln Trail State Memorial on Rt 50 Business in Lawrence County, IL.

Just beyond it was the Lincoln Memorial Bridge, which took me over the Wabash River into Vincennes, Indiana. The bridge marks the location where Lincoln and his father's family crossed the river as they journeyed to Illinois in 1830.

The Lincoln Memorial Bridge in Vincennes, IN.

Despite the various memorials honoring President Lincoln, there were no signs or markers recognizing the "Hoosier State." *I suppose my photo op will have to wait.* I just hope there's an Indiana state sign posted somewhere between here and the Ohio state line or I'm going to be none too pleased.

When I got back onto Route 50, I realized that Bedford (which wasn't the day's original destination, but had become the one I was then striving for) was still roughly 40 miles away, and that there were only two and a half hours until sunset. Riding along the winding country roads when I was forced to get off of Route 50 had cost me considerable time. Still, I had it in my head that I was going to make it to Bedford and set a new personal best for number of miles in a day; so I decided to press on against my own better judgment.

Well, it doesn't take a genius to know that this ended up being a bad decision which left me out on the road after sundown. Had this been a well-lit road or even a straight one, it would have been manageable. This stretch of Route 50 however, was a narrow, twisting course with no streetlights. Now, I did have my headlight, which helped a little, but visibility was limited, making for a long (hour and a half long), stressful ride.

With some hard work, a bit of luck, and a lot of prayers, I managed to make it to Bedford in one piece and in the process learned just how dangerous it is to bike on unfamiliar roads at night. Even though I was excited to have made it there safely and to have put together a banner day mileage-wise, I recognized how foolish I had been. By pushing it like I did, I unnecessarily put myself in harm's way. Moving forward, I have to be more careful; mileage marks and personal achievements are not what this journey is about.

As coincidence or fate – depending on which philosophy you subscribe to – would have it, earlier in the day one of my great friends from college, Kevin Lewis, sent me an encouraging text message (as he so often does). It included a line from a Pearl Jam song, "And he who forgets ... will be destined to remember." Those words couldn't have been any more appropriate for this day because if I forget the valuable lesson I just learned, I very well may be destined to make the same mistake again. And next time I might not be so fortunate.

## Day 30 (10/7/13): Bedford, IL to Versailles, IN [72 miles]

Despite a good night's rest and a big breakfast, it didn't take but a few miles for me to realize that I was running on an empty tank. Century rides are hard enough, but what I did yesterday by pushing it as far as I did was strenuous on a whole other level. Couple that with the stress of riding at night, I was completely worn down.

View from Rt 50 near Bedford, IN.

As I sluggishly pedaled along Route 50, I came across a small pack of rabid dogs. Well, maybe they didn't actually have rabies, but the way they charged toward me made me think they did. Luckily, a chain link fence restrained them unlike those angry German Shepherds I encountered last week. Still, it was unnerving to see dogs racing after me again. The really frustrating thing about this is it seems to happen all the time these days. And, when I say that, I literally mean it happens ... all ... the ... time. Now, I know it has to do with a dog's love for chasing fast moving objects, but come on already, I'm not moving that fast, especially today.

Rabid dogs with razor-sharp teeth aside, the ride was quite picturesque. The leaves on the trees were unveiling their fall colors, and the wheat in the fields had a rich golden-brown hue that I had not yet seen. Although we're already a couple of weeks in, this was the first time I felt as though autumn was truly upon us. And a welcome sight it was, especially when I think back to those scorching hot summer days in the desert.

Later in the day, I called Ida to wish her a happy birthday. That's right, it's my big sister's b-day. She turned 30 *again* if you were wondering. I joke, but she really doesn't look a day over 30. While we were on the phone, she informed me that Alan Faneca would like to meet me in Pittsburgh to do some television and radio interviews. I couldn't have been more excited when she told me the news. Alan and his wife Julie, who have already contributed so much to *Crossing America For A Cure* by offering to match every dollar raised, are now going to help spread the word by reaching out to the media. Their support of this event has been incredible.

Day 30, though physically tough, brought with it a birthday celebration (albeit over the phone), fantastic news, and a new mileage total of over 2,200. More than two thirds of the journey down, the final third to go. That's a pretty darn good day if I do say so myself.

View from Rt 50 near Bedford, IN.

# Day 31 (10/8/13): Versailles, IN to Cincinnati, OH [68 miles]

It was a really cold morning, the coldest one yet. I knew I'd have to deal with cold weather on this journey and even packed clothes for such occasions, but most of those got discarded several states back. Don't shake your head. Hauling around 50 pounds of gear on a bicycle is no easy feat. There were days when fatigue and frustrations were particularly high and I thought it best to lighten the load; and literally did so by tossing stuff into dumpsters.

Well, at some point, I found myself screaming and pedaling as fast as I could in an effort to keep warm. Lord only knows why I was screaming. I guess I heard somewhere that it helps get the blood flowing. I'm not sure if it actually works, but it sure does make you look like you have a screw loose. One thing that definitely did help though was riding in the sunlight. It's funny because during most of this trip I'd begged for clouds, trees, or anything that would provide cover. Thank goodness, by late morning the temperature had started to rise, so I was able to back off the sprints, giving my legs (and my lungs) a rest.

Around noon, I reached the Ohio state line. Yet, before entering "The Buckeye State," I crossed the road, took pics and shot video in front of the Indiana state sign since the darn thing had eluded me when I first arrived.

Al DeCesaris in front of the Indiana sign on Rt 50 in Greendale, IN.

I then went through the same routine just a stone's throw up the road in front of the Ohio state sign. Thus, the same bad hair in both pictures. With appearances in states 9 and 10 properly documented (or documented as well as one can with a camera phone and a couple of road signs), I contently pedaled off.

Al DeCesaris in front of the Ohio sign on Rt 50 in North Bend, OH.

Not long after, I met Hamed, who apparently is also biking across the U.S. We chatted for a bit and swapped funny stories before continuing on. May his ride be safe and, as I now know the significance of the Irish blessing (thanks to that relentless Kansas wind), may the wind be always at his back.

Getting into Cincinnati, my destination for the day, was no easy feat. I found myself in a sticky situation just before reaching the city proper. With concrete barriers on my right and cars rolling by on my left (just inches away from me), I knew I wasn't safe and pulled over at the first opportunity I got. Luckily, right where I pulled over there was an exit to a less congested road that ran along the Ohio River. As I pedaled along, I passed Paul Brown Stadium (home of the NFL's Bengals) and Great American Ball Park (home of MLB's Reds), and enjoyed spectacular views of the Cincinnati skyline and the Ohio River. I was also afforded the opportunity to ride through the city's beautiful riverfront parks. It was a welcome respite from the chaos I had experienced earlier.

The Cincinnati skyline from Mehring Way in Cincinnati, OH.

Leaving the city, however, made getting into it seem like a piece of cake. I found myself in several extremely dangerous predicaments as I tried to navigate State Route 32 during rush hour. High-congestion, concrete barriers, and a nonexistent shoulder had me riding my bike in the dirt and rocks alongside an on-ramp and, at one point, even forced me to abandon the road altogether and ride through a road construction site. It was terribly stressful and quite possibly the worst couple of hours I've endured thus far. It seems no matter the size or layout, big cities are a disaster to get in and out of on a bicycle.

# Day 32 (10/9/13): Cincinnati, OH to Piketon, OH [76 miles]

What a difference a day can make. With traffic at a minimum (most of the vehicles were headed west into Cincinnati) and the road construction site safely behind me, there were no traces of the chaos I'd suffered the previous day. In some ways, it was hard to believe this was the same stretch of State Route 32 East, though it most definitely was; days like yesterday aren't easily forgotten.

The East Fork of the Little Miami River from SR 32 near Batavia, OH.

After several hours of steady, peaceful riding, I stopped at a convenience store and was approached by a guy named TJ. He had seen my cycling jersey with the *Crossing America For A Cure* logo on the chest and back, and asked me about the cause. After telling him about it, he informed me that he was familiar with Sturge-Weber Syndrome through his work as an Emergency Medical Technician. He also confided that he too suffers with seizures, which is one of the many health complications associated with Sturge-Weber Syndrome.

I then learned how his condition has negatively impacted his life. It was sad to hear. Not only do individuals like TJ have to struggle with their illnesses, but they also have to deal with the way others perceive and treat them. Talking with TJ reminded me how important it is to create awareness about seizures as well as the other aspects of Sturge-Weber Syndrome. By creating awareness, we can help people recognize Sturge-Weber Syndrome, tear down the stigma associated with this disorder, engender acceptance of those suffering with it, and foster and advance medical research and treatment.

Although treatment at the present time is limited, earlier this year Anne Comi, M.D., Jonathan Pevsner, Ph.D., Douglas A. Marchuk, Ph.D. and their team of medical researchers discovered the genetic cause of Sturge-Weber Syndrome. I can't stress enough the importance of their discovery and the positive changes it will bring to both treatment and the efforts to find a cure.

The rest of the day was uneventful and went by rather quickly. Before I knew it, I had reached the village of Piketon, my destination for the day. After my customary "I made it safely" phone call and a shower (which included, as always, the tiresome hand-washing of my cycling outfit), my dinner arrived – a large cheese pizza with grilled chicken. (Don't act surprised, you know it's how I roll these days.) The delivery guy, Brett, saw my bike in the room and asked where I was headed and what I was doing. Not missing the opportunity, I told him about *Crossing America For A Cure* and Sturge-Weber Syndrome, and asked him to help spread the word. As my conversation with TJ reminded me, creating awareness is of vital importance.

Al DeCesaris on SR 32 near Piketon, OH.

# Day 33 (10/10/13): Piketon, OH to Athens, OH [67 miles]

Today I rode in honor of Paul Siegel, a Towson University student and fellow Marylander. Although I haven't met Paul yet, I know from our communications and the fundraising page he set up on the *Crossing America For A Cure* website that he's determined to create positive change for everyone suffering with Sturge-Weber Syndrome. I also know Paul plans to become a writer and spread the word about Sturge-Weber Syndrome by telling his story of how living with the disorder affects him. Paul's determination and commitment to the cause are truly inspiring.

Even though I was looking forward to riding for Paul, I got off to a late start, and not by just a few minutes. I was so delayed working on yesterday's blog entry (which I didn't manage to finish the previous night) that the front desk attendant at the motel called my room to remind me that it was time to check out. It seems some days are just harder than others to get the show on the road.

Not far into the ride, I called my brother Michael to go over the blog entry I had just written. Over the past couple of weeks we've developed a nice little system, which has Michael reviewing and editing each entry prior to posting it on our website and Facebook page. He's my editor-in-chief, if you will. Without Michael's help, my blog would be a disjointed, jumbled mess.

In the early afternoon, I saw an Amish man in a field tending to his crops and stopped to have a look. It's not that I've never seen an Amish person before, but after riding through the countryside for the better part of the last two days with little to see other than farms and woodland, anything outside of the norm grabs my attention (especially a guy with a long beard, wearing plain dress clothes, suspenders, and a wide-brimmed straw hat). Now, whether the Amish man appreciated my interest in him was debatable. After taking about the tenth picture of him, I got the feeling I needed to move along or I was going to have to help him raise a barn.

View from SR 32 near Beaver, OH.

Later in the day, my good friend and the designer of the *Crossing America For A Cure* website, Shawn Vernon called to see how I was doing. Although Shawn and I had spoken almost daily in the weeks leading up to my departure (as we worked to get the website up and running), we hadn't had a chance to talk since I set out. Shawn told me how excited he was for me and how amazed he was by the enormity of my endeavor. His enthusiasm and encouragement brought a smile to my face and had me laughing. I guess, despite all of our conversations prior to my departure, he hadn't completely grasped what I was setting out to do. It was understandable though, because even I hadn't fully comprehended just how big of an endeavor riding a bicycle across America would be until I got started.

View from SR 32 near Albany, OH.

Despite the late start this morning, I put together a 65+ mile day, in honor of Paul, and safely reached my destination of Athens, Ohio before nightfall. Although I still have a ways to go, I am now starting to see the light at the end of the tunnel and look forward to seeing old friends like Shawn and new ones like Paul when the journey is complete. Their support and encouragement have been tremendous and have helped me each step of the way. Well, each pedal stroke to be exact.

# Day 34 (10/11/13): Athens, OH to St. Mary's, WV [68 miles]

I have to admit, this whole cycling thing has really grown on me. I guess after 2,400+ miles it was bound to happen. Still, there are some things about it that I will never fully embrace. One of those is the apparel you're supposed to wear while riding. They (whoever they are) say it's aerodynamic, moisture wicking, protective, and much more comfortable than traditional workout clothes. Although I tend to agree with most of what "they" say, I can't stress enough how awkward it is to walk into a convenience store in skin-tight spandex.

And then there's the cream you're supposed to put on your backside to prevent chafing and irritation. The product I've been using is aptly called Butt'r. All right now, I can hear you all laughing, but have no doubt; if you were riding as much as I am, you'd be using it too. Like brushing my teeth and putting on suntan lotion, *liberal* application of Butt'r has become part of my daily routine. Unfortunately, my brain must have been a little foggy this morning because the Butt'r ended up on my face instead of the suntan lotion. Not the best way to start the day, but I suppose it could have been worse. The Butt'r could have ended up on my toothbrush.

Not long into my ride, I spoke to one of my best friends from childhood and the *Crossing America For A Cure* de facto in-house counsel, Adam Cizek. (Yep, yet another unpaid position I've forced upon one of my friends.) Seriously though, Adam and I have known each other since we were kids, and he has been supporting my efforts ever since. Just this year, he helped my family establish *Celebrate Hope Foundation, Inc.* (the non-profit charitable organization that is hosting this fundraising endeavor) and has personally helped raise a considerable amount of money for the cause. So you see, contrary to popular belief, lawyers have hearts too.

Al DeCesaris in front of the West Virginia sign on the Parkersburg-Belpre Bridge in Belpre, OH.

The day's ride took me into the wild and wonderful state (or so the sign says) of West Virginia. It's the state where my other childhood best friend Bob Stanger was born and spent his early years. Despite now calling

Maryland his home, Bob still spends a fair amount of time in West Virginia and knows its backcountry well. So after crossing the Ohio River and entering the "Mountain State," I gave my old friend a call to get a little insight on the area. Surprisingly, Bob didn't have a clue where I was. Apparently, Route 2 along the Ohio River is off the beaten path (and that's saying something 'cause in my opinion the whole state is off the beaten path). Even so, notwithstanding its twists and turns and uncomfortably narrow stretches, the river road was a great route to take as it allowed me to avoid a number of difficult inclines and saved my legs a ton of unnecessary work.

The day ended in the riverside town of St. Mary's and the night in a roadside motel of the same name. One thing I've learned in my 30+ days on the road (other than the fact that spandex is a necessary evil ... oh, and that Butt'r goes on your backside, not your face) is that when a motel takes the name of the town it's located in, it's usually a substandard establishment. Although I can't say it's the worst motel I've stayed in – a few others will be fighting for that honor – I think I would rather have stayed the night in the Bates Motel than this place.

# Day 35 (10/12/13): St. Mary's, WV to Wheeling, WV [67 miles]

Although I've been traveling east nearly the entire way, today I found myself heading north into West Virginia's northern panhandle. Not moving in an easterly direction felt as though I wasn't making progress. Yet, following the Ohio River north made sense since it got me closer to Pittsburgh, my next major destination, while sparing me the climbs of West Virginia's mountainous terrain. So I followed Route 2 North for most of the day and enjoyed a flat track through the scenic Ohio River Valley with tall rock walls on my right and the tranquil blue waters of the Ohio River on my left and, in the distance, low mountains with woodlands of perennial greens and the oranges and reds of autumn.

View from Rt 2 near Moundsville, WV.

View from Rt 2 near Moundsville, WV.

Even though the day's ride was only about 65 miles (I'm not really sure when I started thinking a 65-mile ride was such a simple task), I found myself struggling as though it was my first day on the road. I quickly realized it was because I hadn't eaten much before I started out. Over the course of the last month, I have gotten into a good routine of eating a hearty breakfast of waffles, pancakes, oatmeal, eggs, bacon, bagels, muffins, fruit, and whatever else I can get my hands on. Food equals fuel, and I need as much as I can get to bike 8-10 hours a day. Needless to say, the *fine establishment* I stayed in last night didn't offer anything to eat and there were no decent options in town. So I inhaled a half dozen energy bars and managed to muster up enough energy to keep the legs pumping. Although the "bar binge" worked (more or less), it became quite apparent to me that breakfast *is* the most important meal of the day, especially when you're biking across America.

That afternoon, while I rode down a hill, a train came barreling up alongside of me on the flat strip of land between the road and river. As the train ran along the tracks, I shifted gears and pedaled as fast as I could, trying my best to keep pace with it. Thanks to the downward slope of the hill, I was actually able to do so for a while, but eventually the road leveled out and the train flew by me. On my journey, I've seen dozens of trains thunder across the countryside, but I hadn't experienced anything like this. Racing alongside a moving train was quite a rush.

Not long before reaching my motel in Wheeling (which, I'm happy to say, serves breakfast every morning), a couple of motorcyclists rolled past me. Like most bikers I've come across during my journey, they gave me a thumbs-up and a nod of the head. It's cool how encouraging these guys and gals have been. If there's a bikers club out there for cross-country travelers, I bet they'd vote me in ... at least as an honorary member. I may have to trade in the spandex for leather though.

# Day 36 (10/13/13): Wheeling, WV to West Newton, PA [55 miles]

After a big hot breakfast of somewhere in the neighborhood of 2,000 calories (like I said, food equals fuel, and I need a lot of it), I got on Route 40 East and headed toward the Pennsylvania state line. It felt good to be going east again, though, I must admit, I was a little irritated. Within my view most of the morning was Interstate 70, a flat parallel road, which surely would have made for a much easier ride. But, of course, non-motorized traffic was prohibited on the interstate so I was forced to deal with the steep climbs of the old highway. Even more frustrating was the fact that, when I reached the "Keystone State," Route 40 didn't have a sign welcoming me. If you recall, this happened when I crossed into Indiana as well, and I'm still mad about it. To bike hundreds of miles from one state to the next with nothing to mark your achievement is demoralizing.

Later in the day, as I was struggling with the ups and enjoying the downs of the mountainous terrain, I drew the attention of a hostile canine, who (as you probably guessed) quickly gave chase. For those who have been keeping up with my ramblings, you know how little I like dogs roaming free (fences or leashes please) and how little they like me. Well, my ferocious "Nooooo!" scream, which managed to back down a couple of German Shepherds earlier in the trip, didn't work so well this time. Thankfully, I was able to outrun Cujo as I flew down the backside of a hill. However, I know if that had happened while I was climbing the hill instead of descending it, I probably would have ended up in the back of an ambulance with dog bites on my butt.

As I moved farther east, the terrain got more and more difficult and the wind started to pick up, making for extremely difficult riding. At one point, as I was standing pedaling up a steep incline, I noticed a herd of cows in a field off to the side of the road. Although I had been told never to stop in the middle of a climb, I foolishly did just that to take a picture. When I started pedaling again I couldn't get my feet around quickly enough to gain momentum, and ended up losing my balance and crashing to the ground. As you know, this wasn't the first time I've done this, but that made it no less painful, and no less embarrassing, even though it happened in front of a herd of cattle.

The rest of the day proved no easier. The climbs were long, steep, and frequent. Just to make things more interesting, at some point in the afternoon my cell phone died. Needless to say, without my iPhone navigation and the cycling app I've come to rely on, I had no idea how much farther I needed to go to reach my destination of West Newton, nor did I know whether my family had found accommodations for me. All I could do was continue pedaling east, so that's exactly what I did. In a town I passed through, I came across a kid who asked if I was on the *Tour de France*. Now, I'm not sure if he was serious or messing with me, but either way it was hilarious and brought light to what had become a stressful situation.

When I finally arrived in West Newton, I found a pizza shop where I was able to charge my phone. After a call to my family, I learned that a room had been booked for me. There was just one *little* problem. The motel they found was 12 miles away, which on this rangy terrain would have meant another hour and a half of riding. After a minor meltdown (okay, maybe a major one), they called back to let me know that my younger brother Michael had just found a bed and breakfast in West Newton with availability. I couldn't have been any more relieved to hear those words, or any more thankful for Michael's efforts, because I don't think I had another 12 miles in me. Actually, after today's Appalachian adventure, I don't think I had another two in me.

View from Rt 136 near Eighty Four, PA.

# Day 37 (10/14/13): Pittsburgh, PA

I woke to cloudy skies and a forecast of rain, though it didn't matter to me. Today I was going to Pittsburgh where I would enjoy some much needed rest and relaxation before meeting up with 9-time NFL Pro Bowler and Super Bowl XL Champion Alan Faneca tomorrow to do media outreach. Before heading out, I enjoyed a delicious breakfast and had the pleasure of chatting with Rob and Mary, the innkeepers of Bright Morning Bed & Breakfast, and a few fellow bicycle travelers. Even though I ended up at their B&B by chance, Rob and Mary's hospitality (and the superb food they served) made my time there a worthwhile experience.

Shortly thereafter, I loaded my bike and gear into an SUV, which the Faneca family had been kind enough to send for me, and was driven to Pittsburgh. While the driver navigated the rangy roads, I started to realize that this mountainous terrain, which I had gotten a heavy dose of yesterday, might be the last of which I would have to face. Had I followed my original plan (which was to bike the *Adventure Cycling Association's TransAmerica Trail*), I would have been battling the mountains days ago and would undoubtedly be doing so for days to come. But severe rains and difficult elevations forced me to abandon the *TransAmerica Trail* before I even got on it. I'm thankful that Ida completely reworked the route and has been guiding me across the country ever since. For the next 300 miles or so, "Ida's Route" will have me riding on bike paths safe from speeding cars and crazy inclines. Short of any unforeseen problems, I'll be skirting the mountains and their torturous climbs the rest of the way.

When I arrived in the Steel City, I was immediately taken by how nice it is. Not that I didn't expect it to be. I had heard good things from a number of people, but I had no idea how cool the city of Pittsburgh actually is. The riverfront stadiums, the parks and green spaces, the promenades along the rivers, and the three rivers themselves (the Ohio, the Monongahela, and the Allegheny) make for one impressive city.

The Pittsburgh skyline from the Water Steps in Pittsburgh, PA.

Impressive in its own right is the Renaissance Pittsburgh Hotel, which just so happens to be where I'm staying for the night (compliments of Will Futch, one of my best friends from High School). Of course, any *hotel* would be fantastic compared to the roadside *motels* I've been staying in, but this place is something special. I couldn't be more delighted and appreciative to be able to spend a rest day there.

Still, I couldn't sit in a hotel room all day long, so I ventured out to explore the downtown area, known as the Golden Triangle, and had lunch in Market Square at a place Will recommended, Primanti Bros. The second I entered the old school sandwich shop, saw the crowds, and smelled the food, I knew I was in for a treat. I went with one of their signature sandwiches, a Pastrami and cheese topped with French fries, coleslaw, and tomatoes ... not the healthiest thing on the menu, but boy was it good. I then walked around the North Shore, a neighborhood on the north side of the Allegheny River, passing by PNC Park (home of MLB's Pirates) and Heinz Field (home to both the NFL's Steelers and the Pitt Panthers).

I ended the day kicked back in the Renaissance Pittsburgh Hotel's Concierge Lounge. As I munched on complimentary hors d'oeuvres and sipped complimentary drinks (non-alcoholic, of course), I wondered how on earth I was ever going to get back on my bike after being spoiled like this.

# Day 38 (10/15/13): Pittsburgh, PA

In the morning, I met Alan Faneca in the lobby of my hotel. As I've stated before, Alan and his wife Julie have been amazing in their support of our efforts and, in honor of their daughter Anabelle, who suffers with Sturge-Weber Syndrome, are matching every dollar we raise. In addition, the Faneca family arranged interviews with Pittsburgh television and radio stations to help spread the word about the cause.

Alan Faneca and Al DeCesaris at Point State Park in Pittsburgh, PA
(photo courtesy of Meredith Blake Matthews).

After catching up with Alan, we headed over to Point State Park, which sits at the confluence of the Allegheny and Monongahela rivers, forming the Ohio River. There, we met Meredith, the public relations director who organized the interviews. She took a few photos of us, with the Allegheny River and Heinz Field as a backdrop, and helped with the WPXI TV interview, which went off (dare I say before I've even seen it?) without a hitch.

After a quick stop back at the hotel to change clothes (the spandex cycling ensemble was required for the TV interview, but there was no way in the world I was going to walk around in it all day long), Alan and I made our way over to the two radio stations, which were conveniently located in the same building. The first interview was a recorded segment with KDKA 1020 AM. The second was a live broadcast with Starkey, Miller & Mueller of 93.7 FM The Fan, a popular sports talk radio station. Both interviews went extremely well, and the hosts couldn't have been friendlier, though our time there didn't come without some teasing. Apparently, you shouldn't wear a Washington Redskins t-shirt in Steelers Country.

Afterward, Alan took me to one of the city's finest steakhouses for a thick, juicy filet and a monster portion of bread pudding. Suffice it to say, I did some serious damage in that place. Who'd have thought I could eat as much as (actually more than) a former NFL offensive lineman. I guess a cross-country bike trip works up one hell of an appetite.

That evening, while lounging around the Renaissance Pittsburgh Hotel (which, by the way, the Faneca family generously booked for me for the night), I heard on the news that meteorologists were calling for light rain for tomorrow. I had decided before beginning my journey that for safety reasons I wouldn't bike in the rain. Yet, I knew if I were to take tomorrow off (for what would be a third day in a row), it would be awfully difficult to get going again. It was already going to be hard enough after two days of leisure. So I have decided, rain or no rain, tomorrow I'm back on the bike.

# Day 39 (10/16/13): West Newton, PA to Meyersdale, PA [84 miles]

When I woke in the morning, a light rain was falling, prompting me to rethink my approach to the day's ride. I was adamant I wasn't going to take off yet another day, but I wasn't really equipped to ride in the rain either. So, before leaving Pittsburgh, I made a quick stop to purchase the essential outerwear, which amounted to a $10 poncho. Ok, so maybe it wasn't exactly "top of the line" rain gear, but I figured it was better than what I had, which was next to nothing.

Because of the lousy weather the drive back to West Newton (where I'd left off at a couple of days prior), took longer than expected, but it was a pleasant and informative ride. My driver, Mark, was a wealth of knowledge and gave me great insight into Pittsburgh and its history. By the time we reached West Newton, I was an even bigger fan of the Steel City, and I was grateful the rain had let up.

The bicycle-friendly town of West Newton straddles some unpronounceable Pennsylvania river (the Youghiogheny for those keeping track at home) and the Great Allegheny Passage, a 150-mile rail-trail that runs from Pittsburgh to Cumberland, Maryland. The GAP, as it's also known, is a crushed limestone trail, free of vehicular traffic and steep mountain climbs; actually, it's free of climbs altogether. It was an amazing find. Another well-deserved thanks to my sister (and navigator) for locating it. From Cumberland I'll *hopefully* follow the C&O Canal Towpath another 185 miles to Washington, D.C. That part of the trip is predicated on whether the government shutdown ends in the next couple of days because the Towpath is a national park, and at the present time it's closed along with the Federal Government. Terrible timing, I know. However, short of a police barricade, I'm getting on it.

View from the Great Allegheny Passage near Connellsville, PA.

A bit before noon, I came upon a maintenance crew from the Department of Conservation doing repair work on the GAP. Kevin, the manager of the crew, introduced himself and informed me that the trail was closed beyond that point for repairs and that I would have to turn back. *Turn back? Is he serious? I'm not doing that!* I thought. I resolved to walk my bike in the grass and mud on the side of the trail if I had to. Lucky for me, it didn't come to that. It seems Kevin and some of the other guys had seen the TV interview Alan Faneca and I did yesterday and were just having a little fun with me. After fits of laughter (mainly on their part) and a sigh of relief (wholly on mine), the men congratulated me on my efforts and wished me well.

View from the Great Allegheny Passage near Ohiopyle, PA.

The rest of the day was quiet and peaceful. Well, with the exception of one minor incident. In the late afternoon, as the clouds started to dissipate, I realized I was riding toward the setting sun. The one rule I had this entire trip was, *when in doubt, go east.* Needless to say, it caused a slight panic and had me wondering how I had gotten turned around. I soon realized it was just the result of a bend in the trail. And as the trail swung back around, I was again heading east. Of course, I had to double (and triple) check the compass app on my phone to be certain.

View from the Great Allegheny Passage near Meyersdale, PA.

Today's ride was in honor of Anabelle Faneca, which was fitting in light of all that the Faneca family has done for me the past couple of days. Despite a few unsettling moments, the 80+ mile ride to Meyersdale went rather smoothly. Probably the biggest obstacle of the day was trying to find a place to eat in the old (and eerily sleepy) coal-mining town of Meyersdale. Yet, Albright's Videos & More, a DVD and VHS cassette rental store (who knows maybe they even have Betamax tapes in there), came through with their "& More" which included hot oven-baked pizza … which was surprisingly good.

# Day 40 (10/17/13): Meyersdale, PA to Little Orleans, MD [78 miles]

After scarfing down a carb-packed breakfast, I made my way back onto the Great Allegheny Passage. The sun was hidden behind ominous dark clouds and, as was the case yesterday morning, a light rain fell. Thank goodness, my cycling jacket (of the obnoxious neon-yellow variety) was enough to keep me dry because I was not convinced my fancy new $10 poncho was up to the challenge.

After an hour of weaving between low mountains and through dense woodlands, I came upon the Eastern Continental Divide, the ridgeline separating the Gulf of Mexico Watershed from the Chesapeake Bay Watershed (or so the sign marking its location told me). Just a ways farther down the trail was Big Savage Tunnel, an old railroad tunnel that cuts through the heart of Big Savage Mountain. Both the mountain and the tunnel take their name from surveyor John Savage, who, as legend and the ever-so-reliable website Wikipedia have it, nearly fell victim to cannibalism – escaping, presumably, by the skin of his teeth. (Pardon the pun, but I just can't help myself.)

Big Savage Tunnel from the Great Allegheny Passage near Meyersdale, PA.

My ride through Big Savage Tunnel was exciting but also a bit unnerving. Built to accommodate only a single-track for the now defunct Western Maryland Railway, the abandoned railroad tunnel was uncomfortably narrow and icy cold. Although lights were mounted on the arched ceiling throughout, they failed to fully illuminate the passageway, creating an alternating pattern of light and dark that seemed to go on and on and on. It was reminiscent of a mine, which made me feel as though the farther into it I rode, the deeper into the bowels of the earth I was going. Before long, I caught sight of the opening at the other end and soon emerged to warm, dry air and an amazing view of a lush, serene valley surrounded by wooded mountains of fiery red, burnt and blazing orange, and deep forest green. It was a sight to behold, and well worth the price of admission (which just so happened to be one creepy old tunnel).

View from the Great Allegheny Passage near Meyersdale, PA.

Just beyond it was a stone pillar marking (on one side) the location of the Mason-Dixon line and (on the other) the line between the states of Pennsylvania and Maryland. As I snapped my pics – you know I can't cross a state line without taking the requisite selfies – I was overcome by a wave of emotion, for Maryland is the home of Ocean City (the final destination of this 3,000+ mile bicycle journey), as well as my home state. Even though I knew there was still work to be done (roughly 350 miles of it), my arrival into Maryland made me feel as though I was just about finished.

Al DeCesaris in front of the pillar marking the line between Pennsylvania and
Maryland on the Great Allegheny Passage near Frostburg, MD.

Not long after, I arrived in the city of Cumberland and came to the end – or the beginning depending on which way you're going – of the Great Allegheny Passage. I then got onto the C&O Canal Towpath, which (thanks to the end of the government shutdown) had just re-opened that morning. Despite the benefit of not having to deal with winding country roads and unforgiving mountain climbs, the Towpath presented its own share of problems. It's a rutty, narrow track sandwiched between the Potomac River and the Chesapeake & Ohio Canal, which is poorly maintained and covered with leaves, branches, and tree roots ... a far cry from the Great Allegheny Passage.

Just before 3:00 pm, the rain started to pick back up and I was forced to break out my "state of the art" rain gear. To my surprise, it did the job fairly well, but my progress on the slick, muddy track was sluggish at best. As the sun began its descent, I realized that, at the pace I was traveling, I probably wasn't going to make it to my destination of Hancock before nightfall. That posed a big problem because, from what I had heard, this was one of the most desolate stretches of the Towpath, and there was little if anything between here and Hancock.

While nervously pedaling along, I saw a cyclist standing in front of one of the canal lockhouses. With a welcoming smile, he waved me over as though he was there (at that exact place and time) specifically to help me. He introduced himself as Ben and told me I could find accommodations in Little Orleans, a small town near mile marker 141, roughly 17 miles shy of Hancock. The news really helped calm my nerves and reminded me how fortunate I have been. Nearly every time I've needed help, there has been someone there to lend a hand.

Unfortunately for me, the slow pace I'd been keeping only got worse when I reached the Paw Paw Tunnel. Unlike Big Savage Tunnel, the Paw Paw Tunnel was a dark, dank passage with an extremely narrow walkway perched just a few feet above stagnant water. Although my headlight was fully charged, it only lit about 8-10 feet in front of me, forcing me to walk my bike the entire length of the tunnel.

The Paw Paw Tunnel from the C&O Canal Towpath near Oldtown, MD.

As I crept through the darkness, my imagination ran wild, and I started to doubt whether I was still even on the Towpath. *Had I missed a turn? Was I going the wrong way?* I wondered. I then started to think that the walkway didn't extend the tunnel's entire length, and that I'd have to double back. Eventually, a small point of light in the distance grew larger, and I was relieved to see that the walkway did span the entire way. When I finally made it out, I breathed a huge sigh of relief. And upon realizing that I was still on the Towpath, breathed another. However, the light of day was fading fast.

Not long after, the sun went down and the rain started back up. To make matters worse, I didn't have a cell phone signal (and hadn't for hours). So clearly, I wasn't able to search for accommodations in Little Orleans, nor was I able to send a message to my family asking them to do it.

Over the next hour, I cautiously pedaled along trying my best to avoid the ruts, branches, and roots hidden under the fallen leaves while the canal and the river slowly closed in, leaving the Towpath an exceedingly narrow track. After a brief respite from the rain, the wind started whipping up, the temperature dropped, and the rain began coming down like never before. Within a matter of minutes, I could barely see where I was going. I knew if I didn't stop soon I was going to end up crashing into a tree or riding into the river or the canal. Although there was no shelter to be found, I stopped, hunkered down behind a tree, and did what I could to shield myself from the gusting wind and the pouring rain. I turned my light off to conserve the battery and remained there in complete darkness in the midst of this terrible storm (cold, drenched, and utterly alone), and prayed it would soon let up.

As I listened to the howling wind, the raging river, and the torrential rains, fear set in and my mind started racing yet again. *How long before the Towpath gets washed out? How long before the rising river pulls me in?* It was one of the scariest things I've ever experienced, and one I don't ever want to have to go through again. In time my prayers were answered – the wind subsided and the rain let up, and I was able to continue on.

When I finally reached mile marker 141, I found refuge at Bill's Place, Little Orleans' local watering hole. There, I met a group of folks, who, after suffering through my story, bought me a drink (although I think they would have preferred if it had been a Guinness as opposed to a Gatorade) and commended me on my journey.

My cell phone signal was spotty, but good enough for me to reach Ida. She informed me that she had found a room for me at a bed & breakfast called the Buck Valley Ranch. Not long after, the owner of the B&B, Leon Fox, picked my muddy tail up and brought me back to the ranch. Although it was late, his wife Nadine cooked a mouthwatering meal for me while I showered. After washing all the mud away (believe you me, there was a ton of it), I ate 'til bursting. Leon and Nadine couldn't have been nicer, and being safe (and warm and dry) under their roof after everything that had transpired couldn't have felt any better.

Nadine later wrote to me, "Glad you found us on that dark and stormy night!" But it was I who was glad that Ida had found them ... and that Leon had found me.

# Day 41 (10/18/13): Little Orleans, MD to Harpers Ferry, WV [82 miles]

As I learned last night, Nadine is one hell of a cook. And when I saw the spread her husband Leon prepared for breakfast, I realized he was no stranger to a kitchen either. After devouring another scrumptious feast, I packed my bags (and the PB&J sandwiches they had made me) and said my goodbyes to Nadine and the Buck Valley Ranch. Leon then drove me back to the C&O Canal Towpath and dropped me off where I had left off the previous night.

There was a chill in the air, but the sun was out and working its magic on the muddy path as well as my spirits. A number of cyclists were out and about, actually more than I'd seen the entire trip. It was clearly a new day, making it hard to believe that just last night I had been caught out here all alone in a terrible storm. As I began what was to be an 80+ mile ride to Harpers Ferry, West Virginia, the stress and anxiety of yesterday faded away along with any signs of the storm. Even so, I knew not to forget what had transpired, or more important, how it had come to pass. Deep down I knew that if I had been more diligent I would have made it to Little Orleans before dark (and before the storm broke). But when I'd crossed into Maryland, I started to think the journey was more or less complete and got lulled into a false sense of security. I couldn't let that happen again. There was still a lot of ground to cover (close to 300 miles of it) and I needed to stay focused.

From the moment I set out this morning, I kept my eyes peeled for the Western Maryland Rail Trail, a 20+ mile paved trail that runs parallel to the Towpath. The two routes are separated, at points, by the canal and, at others, by dense woodland. Several people told me where to pick it up. They also told me that if I didn't get on the Rail Trail at that specific spot, I wouldn't be able to get on it until close to its end. Well, despite all my big talk about staying focused, I somehow missed the access point. To add insult to injury, I had to suffer through watching others riding along the flat, smooth track as I bounced and slid around on the bumpy, muddy Towpath. Needless to say, I wasn't happy.

After a half dozen frustrating miles, I found a break in the woodland where it appeared I could cross over and get onto the Rail Trail and jumped at the chance (or, more accurately, cautiously walked my bike across a soggy channel at the chance). For the next hour or so I made great time and enjoyed the company of other riders. But, before I knew it, the Rail Trail came to an end and spat me out a good distance from the Towpath. From there I had to ride on a road for a short distance and then through Fort Frederick State Park (home to a stone fort built in the 1750s to protect settlers during the French and Indian War) before I was able to get back onto the Towpath.

A bit later I came across a waterfall reminiscent of an infinity pool with the waters of the Potomac River vanishing over a vertical drop. I later learned that it isn't a waterfall at all, but an old dam (Dam No. 5, aka Honeywood Dam, to be exact) built in the 1830s to hold back water for the canal. Dam, waterfall, or whatever you call it, it was one of the coolest things I'd seen in a while and warranted a stop (albeit a quick one).

Dam No. 5 on the Potomac River from the C&O Canal Towpath near Clear Spring, MD.

Not long after, I came to Williamsport's Cushwa Basin and saw two guys standing on opposite sides of the Towpath, one with a video camera in front of his face and the other with a camera phone in his hands and a little boy in his arms. *What are they filming?* I wondered as I looked around curiously. Whatever it was, I figured it must be worthy of a photo or two. Yet, when I heard the guy behind the video camera call out to me, I realized it was me they were filming. And, when he lowered the video camera from his face, I saw (keep in mind I'd been on the road for over 40 days and it took a few seconds for it to register in my brain) that it was none other than my brother Joe, and the guy with the kid in his arms was his good friend James. I couldn't believe it. To say that I was shocked would be a colossal understatement.

Al DeCesaris and Joe DeCesaris on the C&O Canal Towpath in Williamsport, MD
(photo courtesy of James Johnson).

After greeting Joe and James and meeting James' 2-year-old son Troy, the guys revealed an even bigger surprise – Joe had brought his bike and was going to ride with me. "Are you serious?" I asked as Joe strapped on his backpack and mounted his bike. Apparently he was, because just a few minutes later James and Troy drove off, and Joe and I headed down the Towpath.

Although Joe and I hadn't seen each other in months, we talk all the time and needed but a few minutes to catch up, and just a few minutes more for the joking and bantering to commence. An hour or two into our ride, the Towpath turned sharply toward the Potomac River, then ran along its banks on raised walkways abutting rock walls past a section of the river known as Big Slackwater. As the historical records reflect, the rock ridge running through this area convinced the canal engineers to divert the boats into Big Slackwater and then have them reconnect with the canal a few miles downstream as opposed to digging through the rock. The Towpath, in turn, was constructed along the diverted course. Riding along Big Slackwater afforded us some amazing views of the river and the rocky cliffs above. And the bends and dips (and lack of guardrails) on the raised walkways made for one wild ride.

Once we got past Big Slackwater, the Towpath returned to its normal course (you know, that rutty, old mule path) adjacent to the C&O canal. At some point, Joe grew bored with it and started pressing me about getting off the Towpath and onto real roads. After studying a map of the area, he worked out an alternate route, which he claimed would allow us to avoid the zigs and zags of the Towpath and shave a few miles off our ride. Although it sounded good in theory, I didn't like the idea of subjecting ourselves to potentially dangerous roads and difficult terrain. Joe, however, kept pressing the issue, so eventually I relented.

Well, it wasn't exactly relenting. It was more like "If you want to suffer through tough climbs and winding country roads (i.e. get a taste of what I've been doing the past 40 days) then so be it." Well, as I'm sure you've already concluded, we may have shaved a few miles off, but we definitely didn't save any time. It might even have taken us longer. And we were forced to deal with several long, steep climbs, a few of which left my big bro pushing his bike up them. I promised Joe I wouldn't photograph him doing that, but I made no such promises with regard to writing about it.

By the time we reached the pedestrian bridge that takes you across the Potomac River and into Harpers Ferry, the sun had nearly disappeared from sight. Yet, in those waning moments, the setting sun illuminated the sky above the historic little town with a billowy yellow light and cast a misty pink glow over the waters of the Potomac and Shenandoah rivers. For you geography buffs out there, Harpers Ferry sits at the confluence of the two rivers. Watching the sun go down and this amazing day draw to a close from that particular spot, with my brother at my side, was something really special. And although I don't like having to ride around after dark (we still needed to find our motel), our timing on this day couldn't have been any more perfect.

The confluence of the Potomac and Shenandoah rivers from The Point in Harpers Ferry, WV.

# Day 42 (10/19/13): Harpers Ferry, WV to Washington, D.C. [65 miles]

After a hearty breakfast, Joe and I set out in the cold of morning under gray skies. We quickly made our way back to the footbridge that crosses over the Potomac River. Before returning to the Maryland side of the river, I stopped to have a last look at "The Land Between the Two Rivers" (the name residents of these parts have given to the historic town of Harpers Ferry), and to take in the view of the confluence of the Potomac and the Shenandoah rivers and the area just beyond it where the states of West Virginia, Virginia, and Maryland meet.

Harpers Ferry from the Appalachian Trail in Harpers Ferry, WV.

Shortly thereafter, we were back on the C&O Canal Towpath and heading south toward our nation's capital. Seeing the Maryland state sign the other day stirred up a lot of emotions since it's my home state and the home of my final destination of Ocean City, and I was fairly certain my arrival in Washington, D.C. would do the same. D.C. was where I was born and where I had spent a considerable amount of time over the past 10 years. In some ways, it felt just as much like home as Maryland did. Well, no matter how "at home" the sights and sounds of D.C. made me feel, I couldn't let my guard down. I have to remain focused until the journey is complete.

A bit before noon, we took a short break so I could record a video message for Liliana Mae Medlock, an independent and perseverant little girl suffering with Sturge-Weber Syndrome. I dedicated my ride today to the 5-year-old Floridian and wanted to let her and her mother, Elizabeth, know how much I appreciated their support and encouragement. I also had the pleasure of watching a video Elizabeth prepared for me, introducing her three lovely daughters, Layla, Liliana Mae (Lily), and Logan, and thanking me for my efforts. It was awesome! The fact that Elizabeth and her children had taken the time to put together this heartfelt video was truly incredible.

As I've stated previously, my goals when I set out on this journey (aside from creating awareness and raising funds) were to give hope to those affected by Sturge-Weber Syndrome and to inspire others to help make a difference. Though I believe to some extent I have accomplished these goals, I didn't realize how much brave and determined individuals like Lily and her mom would end up inspiring me. Despite the challenges Lily faces, by all accounts she's doing well in kindergarten and is exceeding expectations. She's also (like me) an avid fan of Captain America, the Incredible Hulk, and Spider-Man, which (in my book) makes her one very cool kid.

The ride the rest of the day went smoothly (for me at least). Joe, however, struggled with several episodes of severe cramping. Even though it was obvious he was in pain, he didn't complain much and, with the exception of a few breaks to stretch, he pushed on through like a champ.

Blockhouse Point from the C&O Canal Towpath in Darnestown, MD.

The closer we got to D.C. the busier the Towpath became. As we approached Great Falls, a section of the Potomac River where the water cascades over a series of steep, rocky falls, the Towpath was absolutely packed. Having to ride on a narrow, bumpy path among throngs of tourists milling about was a bit annoying, but I guess it was to be expected. It was a pleasant Saturday afternoon in autumn at one of the D.C. metro area's most visited landmarks and, from the little I saw (big bro Joe wouldn't stand for any lollygagging), a sight well worth seeing.

A little over an hour later, we entered D.C. (or the "District of Columbia" for those who prefer to reference it by its formal name). Unfortunately, there's no sign on the Towpath welcoming travelers when they arrive. As you know, I have a picture of myself in front of the state sign of each of the states I've biked through. And although I realize that Washington, D.C. technically isn't a state, to give up on this budding tradition at this point would be ridiculous. So I assured myself that before I left D.C. I'd track down one of those signs and snap a pic of my mug in front of it.

Not long after, Joe and I arrived in the historic neighborhood of Georgetown where our travels on the C&O Canal Towpath came to an end. After stretching our legs, we made our way over cobblestone streets lined with row houses and buildings of 18th and 19th-century architecture, and past high-end shops, boutiques, cafes, restaurants, and bars before arriving at the waterfront along the Potomac River. There, we met up with my old friend Will Futch, who rode his bike over to meet us. From the start, Will has been extremely supportive of the cause, even paying for a couple of hotel rooms for me (and that's hotel with an H). Will was also kind enough to invite me to stay at his home in D.C.

for the night. After handshakes and hugs (man-hugs, that is) we stepped into one of the restaurants by the water to grab a bite to eat.

As the three of us sat there telling stories and catching up, I noticed a few people looking over at me curiously. Typically, I would have been embarrassed to be sitting in a restaurant in my cycling shorts and jersey, but on this day I couldn't have cared less. I'd like to say I'd reached a Zen-like state with regard to my spandex cycling ensemble, but I think it had more to do with the fact that I was starving.

Afterward, we all got back on our bikes and pedaled over to Will's place. As we approached his condominium building, Joe spotted his friend James, whom he had called to come pick him up. Apparently, Joe had had enough bicycling fun, which was understandable. Over the past 30 hours, he had biked approximately 100 miles and, no matter how fit you are, that's no easy feat. When all was said and done, even though Joe and I only got to ride together for a short time, it was a lot of fun, and I was really happy he had joined me.

# Day 43 (10/20/13): Washington, D.C. to Annapolis, MD [41 miles]

In the morning, I pedaled over to the National Mall to meet my family. They live less than 30 miles from D.C., and there was no way we were going to pass up the opportunity to see each other and get some quality photos together in our nation's capital. Shortly after I arrived, my parents and the Heck clan (which included Ida and her girls: Kaitlyn, Julia, and Jenna, and Kaitlyn's friend Allie) came bounding down the street waving and smiling. It was wonderful to see everyone, especially Jenna for whom I had taken on this crazy adventure.

Ida Heck, Jenna Heck, Al DeCesaris at the World War II Memorial in Washington, D.C
(photo courtesy of Ida Heck).

After heartfelt hugs and kisses, we headed over to the National World War II Memorial, which honors the more than 400,000 Americans who died during the Second World War. The memorial is situated on the National Mall between the Lincoln Memorial and the Washington Monument, and its open design allows for amazing views of both. It consists of 56 granite pillars arranged in semicircles around an oval-shaped plaza and a pool with fountains. On opposite sides of the plaza and pool stand two triumphal arches (one represents the campaign on the Atlantic front, the other the campaign on the Pacific). On the west side of the memorial rests Freedom Wall. The wall has 4,048 gold stars, each representing 100 Americans who made the ultimate sacrifice for our country during the war. Inscribed in front of the wall are the words, "Here we mark the price of freedom." Even though I have been to the memorial many times before, gazing upon the emblematic structure never fails to impress me. And reflecting on the sacrifices made by the men and women we proudly call "The Greatest Generation" always leaves me humbled and grateful.

Between touring the memorial and taking pictures, Ida and I put a FaceTime call in to Elizabeth Medlock and her daughter Lily to personally thank them for their support and introduce them to Jenna. Although Ida and I had communicated with Elizabeth several times since we linked up with her last month, our communications were limited to text and video messages, and we had never actually spoken. It was great to finally talk with her and make a personal connection. Sturge-Weber Syndrome may bring terrible hardship to those suffering with it and their families, but it also brings people together. Our new friendship with Elizabeth and her family was a great example of that.

Shortly thereafter, my parents headed out with Jenna. I was to see them later so our parting was quick and painless. My niece Julia and I (her on her shiny new bike and me on my well-broken-in one) then rode over to the Lincoln Memorial. Ida, Kaitlyn, and Allie joined us not long after, and we took photos in front of the neoclassical memorial dedicated to our 16th President, Abraham Lincoln. We then snapped a few pics against a backdrop that included the Reflecting Pool and the Washington Monument, not far from the very spot where Martin Luther King Jr. delivered his seminal "I Have a Dream" speech.

Al DeCesaris in front of the U.S. Capitol in Washington, D.C. (photo courtesy of Ida Heck).

Julia and I then rode our bikes over to the U.S. Capitol, which is located at the east end of the National

Mall. Although it was a short jaunt, it afforded me the opportunity to spend a little quality time with my soccer-star niece. Ida and the other girls met us there, and more photos were taken. We then said our goodbyes, and I pedaled off.

From the Capitol, I headed up to H Street and followed it east through the Atlas District. Not far beyond it, I caught a glimpse of RFK Stadium (the old home of the Washington Redskins where I spent many Sunday afternoons in my youth) before crossing the Anacostia River. I then made my way onto Central Avenue SE and, before I knew it, came to the D.C./Maryland line. As I had hoped, there was a Washington sign there, and with a cell phone snapshot, I maintained my streak before entering Maryland yet again.

Al DeCesaris in front of the Washington sign on
Central Avenue SE in Washington, D.C.

I followed Central Avenue through Prince George's County (where I lived during my childhood) and into Anne Arundel County (where I spent my formative years). As I rode through the community of Davidsonville, I saw a group gathered in front of a market with balloons and a huge sign that read "Congratulations Al on Crossing America For A Cure." As I drew closer, I realized it was my family (my parents Albert and Rose Mary, my aunts Mary and Liz, my cousins Ali, Sarah, and Luca, my grandma Carmela, my sister Ida and her husband Ed, and their children Julia, Kyle, and Jenna) and friends. It was a nice surprise, though I couldn't help but laugh. I'd just seen many of them a few hours earlier and would see most of them again that evening at my parents' house for dinner. What can I say? We're one ridiculously close-knit family.

Al DeCesaris and family on Central Ave in Davidsonville, MD (photo courtesy of Ida Heck).

After the surprise reception, I continued on toward my destination for the day, Sandy Point State Park on the Chesapeake Bay in Annapolis. As I made my way there,

I passed through Annapolis proper and took the opportunity to visit my cousin Tommy and his wife Kristin and meet their new baby boy Dominic. Since we began this crusade, the Vendemia family has supported our efforts and dedicated a significant amount of time and money to the cause. To share a little part of my journey with them and meet the newest addition to their family while doing it was important to me.

The ride the rest of the way was easy, though at one point I started to doubt whether I was going in the right direction. Believe it or not, in all of my years living in the area, I'd never once been to Sandy Point State Park. Fortunately for me, a cyclist happened to ride by and escorted me to the access road that led to the park. Ida arrived a few minutes after me and (as I'm sure you've guessed) conducted yet another photo session. This one had an impressive backdrop, the Chesapeake Bay and the enormous dual-span steel bridge crossing over it (known in these parts simply as "The Bay Bridge").

Al DeCesaris at Sandy Point State Park in Annapolis, MD (photo courtesy of Ida Heck).

I then loaded my bike and gear into Ida's SUV and we started off toward our parent's house where my loving family (and loads of food) awaited. As we made our way, my thoughts turned to Karli Abrantes, the young woman from Pennsylvania whom I had ridden in honor of today. A couple of weeks before I set out, I received an incredibly touching email from Karli's mother Alison thanking me for creating *Crossing America For A Cure* and wishing me good health and the best of luck. Since the start of this journey, it has been encouragement and support such as this that have kept me going and made this arduous task achievable. Although this day was filled with a number of memorable family moments, riding for Karli and being blessed with her and her mother's encouragement and support made this day a special one.

# Day 44 (10/21/13): Stevensville, MD to Georgetown, DE [61 miles]

Today I rode in honor of Jenna, my beautiful and energetic nine-year-old niece, who was the inspiration behind this bicycle journey. Even though I was eager to knock out the last 100 miles and bring this wild ride to a close, when Ida suggested visiting Jenna's school (Davidsonville Elementary School) and speaking to her and her classmates about my journey and the cause, I thought *what better way to create awareness about Sturge-Weber Syndrome?* And *what better way to celebrate Jenna's special day with her?*

When I rolled into the school parking lot, I was greeted by dozens of cheering students, several of the teachers, and even some of the students' parents. Everyone was cheering, clapping, and waving homemade signs in the air. It was one heck of a reception. Even though Ida had told me that the school had planned something big, I was taken aback by the enormity of it all.

As I came to a stop in front of Jenna and her classmates, I must not have been focused on what I was doing because I ended up unclipping my left foot and leaning to the right. With a ton of nervous energy (and a bit of luck), I managed to catch my balance *just* before toppling over. I don't think the kids realized just how close I came to falling, but judging from the look on Ida's face she definitely did. I can only imagine how hard the kids would have laughed. I'm actually laughing about it as I type this.

Present among the students' parents was my old friend Bob Stanger. From the very day I told him about my plan to bike across the country, he (after, of course, telling me I was crazy) has been extremely supportive. Through his company, Stanger Insurance Group, he has provided a great deal of financial support as an event sponsor. He and his wife Kimmie even rearranged their busy schedules so Bob could ride with me today and tomorrow.

Bob Stanger and Al DeCesaris at Davidsonville Elementary School in Davidsonville, MD (photo courtesy of Kimmie Stanger).

Bob (proudly wearing the *Crossing America For A Cure* cycling jersey I provided) greeted me with a big smile and a hug. It was great to see him, and it meant a lot to me to know he would be riding with me the rest of the way. I'm very fortunate to have such loyal and supportive friends as Bob & Kimmie, and I'm extremely grateful for their support.

A few minutes later, a humorous "Uncle Al" chant started up and, before long, everyone was joining in on the fun. I'm not sure who initiated that nonsense, but if it was Bob, I may have to take all those kind words back. Well, whoever the guilty culprit was, they got me good. I really can't complain though; it was far less embarrassing than falling off my bike. I should know, I've done that plenty of times before.

Al DeCesaris with Jenna Heck and her classmates at Davidsonville Elementary School in Davidsonville, MD (photo courtesy of Ida Heck).

After the chanting subsided, I joined Jenna at her side and took photos with her and her classmates. I met a few of the teachers and said hello to my parents, Ida and Ed and their son Kyle, Bob's wife Kimmie and their kids Chloe and Mason, and the other parents who had come to welcome me. I was then interviewed by several reporters before being ushered into the school auditorium, where over a hundred enthusiastic children eagerly waited to hear about my journey (or, more likely, were just happy to be out of class).

Ida spoke first, telling the children about Sturge-Weber Syndrome. Our hope is that through education we can create awareness, and that awareness in turn will lead to acceptance of those suffering with the disorder. She did a great job explaining the various health complications associated with it and how they affect Jenna while stressing that medical issues aside, Jenna is no different than any other little girl. For those suffering with medical conditions, acceptance by their peers and society in general is of vital importance.

After being introduced to the children, I explained to them how I was using my bicycle journey across America to help Jenna and all those suffering with Sturge-Weber Syndrome. I wanted to make a difference in their lives, I told them. I went on to point out that we all (including each and every one of them) have the power to make a difference. For obvious reasons, I would love for my journey to bring new supporters to our cause. But, ultimately, my hope is that it will inspire others to help those who are in need, be it a friend, loved one, or even a perfect stranger.

After a long-winded explanation of why I was wearing an absurd spandex getup and sharing tales of my adventures, I fielded some rather interesting questions from the kids. "No, I've never ridden my bike in outer space," I responded to one boy's question. "It's helmet hair … it's kind of like bed-head," I explained to Chloe Stanger after she asked me what was going on with my hair. Eventually, the questions shifted to those subjects that seem to draw the most interest from both kids and adults. What did I eat? Where did I sleep? And, *most important*, where did I go to the bathroom?

After my visit at the school, Ida drove Bob and me to Stevensville (the day's starting point), which was just on the other side of the Bay Bridge. I hated that I wouldn't be able to bike over the bridge, but there was nothing I could do about that. The 4.3 mile steel structure is part of U.S. routes 50 and 301, and anything other than automobile traffic is strictly prohibited. Although I wanted to make it happen, every scenario I dreamed up ended with me getting arrested or, even worse, causing an accident. As Bob and I unloaded our bikes and gear at a Stevensville gas station/convenience store, I reminded myself that this journey wasn't about personal goals or achievements and that taking unnecessary risks and putting myself (and others) in harm's way was the last thing in the world I should be considering. This was a mission for the well-being of Jenna and all those suffering with Sturge-Weber Syndrome, and getting across the country safely was what mattered.

The land east of the Chesapeake Bay is known as Maryland's "Eastern Shore." It's predominantly agricultural, quiet and peaceful, and the terrain is extremely flat. Barring inclement weather, these last 100 miles would be easy, stress-free ones. Yet, the angry dog we encountered a couple of hours into our ride made me reconsider that notion. I immediately tensed up as thoughts of bloodthirsty dogs raced (and chased) through my head. Bob, however, brought light to the situation when he jokingly said, "I don't have to outrun the dog.... I just have to outrun you." To that I laughed hard, though it didn't keep me from quickening my pace until the dog was well behind us.

Al DeCesaris in front of the Delaware sign on Rt 404 near Greenwood, DE.

In the late afternoon, we arrived at the Delaware state line and took a break to snap a few pics and shoot video. Delaware was the 14th state I'd entered and, with only about 50 miles of road ahead of us before returning to Maryland, it would be my shortest ride through any state (unless, of course, you include D.C. in the mix). "The First State" held years (eight and a half to be exact) of great memories for me as an undergraduate at the University of Delaware and later as manager of our family restaurant. There were also a handful of fun summers in good ole Dewey Beach. Despite the fact that it would only be a brief stay, it was good to be back.

Bob and I ended our day at a motel in Georgetown, Delaware, which was generously paid for by Brittney and Phil Hastings, whom I will meet tomorrow. The Hastings are the parents of 22-month-old Stella, who suffers with Sturge-Weber Syndrome. Like the other families I've had the privilege of getting to know during my journey, the Hastings are committed to fighting this devastating disorder and have become ardent supporters of my efforts. I was really looking forward to meeting them and little Stella in the morning and then again at the end of the day in Ocean City, Maryland when this wild ride finally comes to an end.

# Day 45 (10/22/13): Georgetown, DE to Ocean City, MD [39 miles]

Today marked my 45th day on the road, and the last of my journey. It started (after a carb laden breakfast) with a visit to Sussex Technical High School, where the school's Leadership Development Program (LDP) arranged a special reception for me. This was prompted by the LDP students' efforts to create awareness and raise money for Sturge-Weber Syndrome research in honor of Stella Hastings.

Al DeCesaris, Phil Hastings, Stella Hastings at Sussex Technical High School in Georgetown, DE (photo courtesy of Sussex Technical High School).

When Bob and I arrived at the school, we were greeted by the LDP students and their teachers, Brittney and Phil Hastings and their young daughters Layla and Stella, and Bob's friend, Amy, who lives in the area. Also on hand were reporters from the Sussex County Post and WMDT 47 ABC News. After chatting with the students and fielding a few questions from the reporters, I got to spend some time with sweet little Stella, for whom I was riding today.

Bob and I were then escorted into the school where we had lunch with the students and teachers. After eating, I spoke to the students about Sturge-Weber Syndrome, my niece Jenna, and my journey. I also explained to them that we all have the power to make a difference and that when you put your mind to something for the well-being of others you can make it happen, no matter how difficult the task. Through this journey, I am living proof of that. After my talk and a brief question-and-answer session, the students presented me with a Sussex Tech t-shirt and a gift bag for Jenna. It was so nice of them, especially because they had thought of Jenna.

After a quick interview and a few photos, we said our goodbyes, and Bob and I pedaled off. As we made our way down the road, I marveled at how kindhearted the students were and how supportive of the cause they have been. The very thought of how they have been selflessly working to help Stella, Jenna, and all the others suffering with Sturge-Weber Syndrome was remarkable and uplifting. My time with Brittney and Phil was meaningful as well. Their love for their children and their dedication to the cause is truly amazing. I was excited to have met them and to be able to call them my friends (albeit brand new ones), and couldn't wait for Ida and the rest of my family to meet them.

A few hours later, Bob and I stopped at a gas station/convenience store for a couple of Gatorades. I stayed with the bikes while Bob went inside, and I got into a conversation with a lady who asked what I was riding for. As I was telling her about the cause, Bob must have been doing the same thing inside the store because when he came out, he had with him Angie and Dawn, two of the store's employees. The women were interested to hear more about the cause and couldn't have been nicer. Just as I started telling them about Jenna, Ida and Jenna pulled into the parking lot. Apparently, they had seen us as they were driving down the road on their way to Ocean City and pulled over to say hello. Angie was so excited to meet Ida and Jenna that she made a donation to the cause right on the spot. Too bad I didn't have Ida and Jenna with me the entire trip. No doubt we would have raised a lot more money.

An hour or two farther down the road, a vehicle came up behind us and blasted the horn. I can't speak for Bob, but it scared the hell out of me. Yet, as the pickup truck rolled by, I realized it was my cousin Tommy and his son Luca just messing with us. I shook my head with equal parts irritation and relief. Tommy turned around, pulled up next to us, and with a teasing smile told us to "hop on in." To that, we all had a good laugh.

As we made our final approach, I saw a bike path to our right running parallel to the road and pointed it out to

Bob who was pedaling along just a few feet in front of me. Bob must have thought I was telling him to get on it because he crossed in front of me just as we came up on a small overpass. Yet, for whatever reason, he didn't get all the way over and, just a few feet from the start of the overpass guardrail, he swerved back in front of me. I hit the brakes and veered to the left, just barely avoiding his back tire. I was extremely fortunate our tires didn't hit because if they had, I most likely would have gone crashing face-first onto the hard pavement. Can you imagine, after biking all that way, if I had wrecked in the last few miles? How embarrassing would that have been? I never would have heard the end of it.

After laughing our butts off about our near disastrous collision, we turned onto Coastal Highway and crossed the Maryland state line, then entered the resort town of Ocean City. We soon arrived at the Braemar Towers where I had spent summers in my youth and where Ida and her family currently spend theirs. Ida and my parents were there to greet us when we arrived. Before we had even come to a stop, I told them about how Bob had almost wiped me out. I couldn't resist the chance. A little razzing of my old friend was definitely in order.

We then headed down to the beach where Tommy and Luca, my nephew Kyle, my nieces Kaitlyn, Mia, and Jenna, and Jenna's friend Katie were eagerly awaiting my arrival. With my loving and supportive family looking on, I kicked off my shoes, raised my bike over my shoulder, and stepped into the Atlantic Ocean, completing my cross-country bicycle journey. Jenna joined me at the water's edge and, with my little inspiration at my side and a sign in her hands that read "Coast to Coast, 3,088 miles, 45 days, 14 states", we happily posed for the camera.

Al DeCesaris on the beach in Ocean City, MD (photo courtesy of Grant L. Gursky).

Al DeCesaris and family on the beach in Ocean City, MD (photo courtesy of Ida Heck).

Shortly thereafter, photographer Grant Gursky and reporter Elaine Bean from the Daily Times arrived; they took photos and interviewed me. I then mounted my bike and rode to the Greene Turtle Sports Bar & Grille where I received a thundering ovation from a large crowd of supporters as I crossed a makeshift finish line.

Al DeCesaris at the Greene Turtle in Ocean City, MD (photo courtesy of Grant L. Gursky).

After congratulatory hugs, handshakes, and kisses, Councilwoman Margaret Pillas on behalf of Ocean City Mayor Richard W. Meehan presented me with a Proclamation. Reading from it, she said, "... the Town of Ocean City is turning out at the Greene Turtle to give Al DeCesaris, Jenna Heck, and their entire family a big Ocean City Homecoming and to congratulate Al on this tremendous accomplishment." And what a homecoming it was. In addition to the raucous crowd, there were homemade signs, balloons, and banners. They even had my name on the Greene Turtle's marquee. It was awesome and made for a fun, celebratory atmosphere.

Lisa Dennis of the Greater Ocean City Chamber of Commerce presented me with a Certificate of

Appreciation. Even though I had no expectations of receiving such accolades, being recognized like this was a real honor. Newspaper interviews and a live TV interview with WMDT 47 ABC News followed.

Al DeCesaris, Ida Heck, Jenna Heck at the Greene Turtle in Ocean City, MD (photo courtesy of Ida Heck).

I then joined my family and friends inside the Greene Turtle for a wonderful celebration. It was really nice to get to spend time with everyone and finally be able to relax (with no worries about how many miles I'd have to ride the following day). Although I didn't get a chance to thank everyone personally, I was very appreciative that they had come to Ocean City to celebrate this momentous occasion with me.

I suppose with everything going on I never got a chance to eat. Though, before we called it a night Tommy got a couple of pizzas from Pizza Tugos, which just so happens to be my favorite pizza shop in town.

With me, Bob, Ida, and my nieces and nephew gathered around, Tommy lowered his tailgate, tossed the pizza boxes in the bed of his truck, and our "pickup truck pizza party" began. As we polished off one pie, then the next, I told them stories of my adventures on the road.

Reflecting on it now, it's hard to believe I actually biked over 3,000 miles from Santa Monica, California all the way to Ocean City, Maryland. The feat seemed impossible, especially for a guy like me with little training and no real cycling experience. Yet, by the grace of God and with the support and encouragement of family and friends, I was able to successfully complete my cross-country bicycle journey. And, through *Crossing America For A Cure,* I was able to create awareness about Sturge-Weber Syndrome across the country, raise funds to further the efforts to find a cure, inspire numerous individuals to join the fight, and give hope to Jenna and countless others suffering with this devastating neurological disorder.

Al DeCesaris and Jenna Heck on the beach in Ocean City, MD (photo courtesy of Ida Heck).

AUTHOR'S NOTE

Thank you for purchasing and reading *Crossing America For A Cure*. I hope you enjoyed the ride. Through your generous support, we're creating more awareness about Sturge-Weber Syndrome every day, and raising critical funds for medical research.

To further support the cause, please share *Crossing America For A Cure* on social media and recommend it to your family and friends. Also, let them know that ALL profits from the sale of this book fund Sturge-Weber Syndrome research.

Another great way to help is to post a book review online (www.amazon.com and/or www.goodreads.com). Book reviews really help spread the word and, in this case, will help raise greater awareness about Sturge-Weber Syndrome.

Together we are giving hope to those suffering with Sturge-Weber Syndrome and inspiring others to join the fight against this devastating neurological disorder!

With sincere thanks,

Al DeCesaris

## Acknowledgments

A charitable event this ambitious would not have been possible without the help, advice, support, and encouragement of a great number of people. Although it would be near impossible to list them all, I want to take this opportunity to thank as many as I can. I apologize for any misspellings or omissions. I truly appreciate everything everyone did for me and for the cause.

Thank you to those who generously donated to the cause, and to the following companies and individuals who sponsored the event:

Event Sponsors: Greene Turtle of Annapolis, MD and Stanger Insurance Group

Gold Sponsors: Timberlake Homes, Angel Care Network, Lizzy and Mark Lahive, CyberStudios, LLC, and Little Bit Heart

Silver Sponsors: Heidi and Ray Mudd III, Lakeside Title Company, Mark Fletcher, Jody and Warren Hayden, Megan and Curtis Bowcutt, Erin Rix, and Blueprint Custom Homes, LLC

Bronze Sponsors: Environmental Solutions, Inc., Red Octopus Tattoos, Inc., Thomas Hattar, M.D., Little Learners Program, Phil, Brittney, Layla, and Stella Hastings, Natalie and Chris Conte, Lucente Enterprises, JoAnne Dewey and family, Tiffany and Albert Procopio, Dr. Bryan D. and Summerson Springer, Dr. John and Michel Wall, JoAnn and Daniel Wellington, DiNenna Lee CPAs, LLC, Susan and Mike Cannone, Jason Nader, Bill, Sheri, and Hannah Darkow, Thomas Connelly, Kimberly Tirlia, Michelle and Chris Vendemia, Ida and Jim Mabe, Mia Tripodi, Jacqueline and Ken Yates, Annette DeCesaris, Elly Latessa, Lianne and Jeff Caruso, Ricky Hammond, Alexia and John Gallagher

Thank you to the following individuals for their advice and support:

Joanne Dewey, Joey Dewey, Mary Vendemia, Liz Arcuri, Carmela Willingham, Lauren Majewski, Dan Cole, John Ferris, Daniel Wellington, Scott Shelton, Jeff Hollman, Brendan Wills, Teddy Herrera, Bill Stegall, America ByCycle, Stephen McDaniel, Sonny Sukalo, Dave Brulinski, Laurie Rostock, Diana Lambird, John McFarland, Cynthia McKinnon and Elson Miles, Cheryl and Travis Brock, Ginny and Ken Stark, Carrie and Jason Leljedal, Will Futch, Nadine and Leon Fox, Brittney and Phil Hastings, Maria and Sarah Fitzmaurice, Jeff Gunhus, REI of Manhattan Beach, Davidsonville Elementary School, Sussex Technical High School, The Town of Ocean City, MD, Greater Ocean City Chamber of Commerce, and Greene Turtle of Ocean City, MD

Thank you to the following individuals for riding with me:

John Wall, M.D., Brian Allman, Mark Espelien, Joe DeCesaris, Will Futch, Julia Heck, and Bob Stanger

Thank you to those who encouraged me to take on this crazy endeavor ... and to keep pedaling.

A big heartfelt thank you to those brave individuals who inspired me:

Jenna Heck, Anabelle Faneca, Lynn Ray, Paige McGrady, Keegan Deveney, Stella Hastings, Karli Abrantes, Paul Siegel, and Liliana Mae Medlock

Thank you to Julie and Alan Faneca for helping promote this charitable event and for matching every dollar it raised. Your generosity and support are extraordinary.

Thank you to my medical team, Bryan D. Springer, M.D., John Wall, M.D., and John Gallagher, D.P.T., for answering my never-ending barrage of questions and getting me across America in one piece.

Thank you to Grant L. Gursky for photographing the conclusion of my bicycle journey and for allowing the use of those brilliant images in this book.

Thank you to my brother, Michael, for tirelessly reviewing and editing my blog as well as this book.

Thank you to Kathryn Johnson and Sher A. Hart for your advice, support, and editorial services to this book.

Thank you to Shawn Vernon of CyberStudios, LLC for all of your hard work and creativity on the *Crossing America For A Cure* website.

Thank you to my cousins, Elizabeth DeCesaris and Jenna DeCesaris Butler of Little Bit Heart, for your amazing design work on the *Crossing America For A Cure* logo and book cover.

Thank you to my siblings, Ida, Joe, and Michael, for standing by my side through it all.

Thank you to my parents, Albert and Rose Mary, for showing me the way and making it all possible.

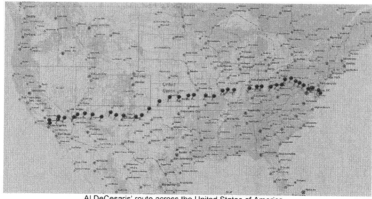

Al DeCesaris' route across the United States of America.

## WORDS OF ENCOURAGEMENT AND APPRECIATION

Al DeCesaris, Ida Heck, their family, and Jenna inspire me so much with this effort to support our work here. We know that so many count on us to help in the present and to discover a better future. We take this journey together – each of us doing all that we can.

Anne Comi, M.D.


Thank you Al for all you are doing!!!! Love following you and your journey!

Julie Faneca


I was just informed of your journey ... and I find myself in tears. It is quite admirable for you to take on such a journey. I received this information as I am a parent of a daughter diagnosed at the age of 14 months with Sturge-Weber.... I just simply want to thank you for creating such an event ... guaranteed to raise human spirit across the country, and I love it.

Alison Furchner


You truly are an inspiration to so SO many people! You are amazing!!! Thank you for making a difference!!!!

Summerson Springer


It was truly a privilege for [my husband] Mark to ride with you out of Albuquerque.... One person can make a HUGE difference – and you have! God bless you!

Lisa Espelien

As someone with Sturge-Weber I could not be more proud of your accomplishments.... Thank you from the bottom of my heart for doing all you can for those with SWS.

Paul Siegel

I love all the knowledge.... I'm smarter after reading your posts.... And tired ... My legs hurt just thinking about it! You rock!!!

Kimmie Graybill Stanger

Thank you for doing this for all the families effected by Sturge-Weber Syndrome. When the doctors find a cure you will have the satisfaction of knowing you played a huge part. We will forever be grateful for all you are doing.

Carrie Leljedal

Even watching from Dublin Ireland with appreciation ... My baby has this [SWS] and care [is] not great here ... Thanks for what you are doing.

Gill Hyland

As a mother [of a child with SWS], I cannot thank you enough for what you are doing. Our family will be praying for your safe travels and look forward to seeing pictures of you crossing the finish line!!! ... Positive thoughts, prayers, and hugs to you ...

Kristy McGrady

Our 8 month old daughter Addyson has SWS.... I would like to express our thanks to you in spreading the word and making people aware of this syndrome.

Vicky Davis

Al, you never cease to amaze me! What you are doing is absolutely amazing! Stay strong and eat your Wheaties ;)

Maureen Moriarty-Orosz

Go Al and Jenna!!! What a team ☺

Jennifer Muñoz Dugan

An Irish Blessing to my Italian friend!
May the road rise up to meet you. May the wind be always at your back. May the sun shine warm upon your face; the rains fall soft upon your fields. And until we meet again, may God hold you in the palm of His hand!! Good luck my friend and brother Al.

John Gallagher

My daughter Liliana was diagnosed with SWS at 3 and we fly to Baltimore from Florida once a year just to see Dr. Comi.... Thank you for your passion to make a difference! We are cheering for you in Northwest Florida!

Elizabeth Medlock

There will forever be a special place in our heart for this incredible man [Al] and his family!

Brittney Hastings

Wonderful accomplishment. It was great to meet you and may God bless your Niece and those who are working on a cure!

Bud Greeley

Your resolve and commitment to Jenna and Sturge-Weber is so inspiring to all of us. Godspeed to you and many blessings!

Cheryl Brock

It is truly amazing what you have accomplished in raising awareness for Jenna and all the others who have SWS. You are a true hero and an inspiration.

Lauren Majewski

Amazing!!! Or rather, Al-Mazing!

Mike Cannone

Congratulations on a ride well ridden. I'm sharing the house tonight with two *Warm Showers* guys.... We talked about you at dinner. You have and will continue to touch lives.... Thanks for letting me be a part of it.

John McFarland

Al, I met you on day 1 and I never had a doubt that you would see this through and that it will bring you and your cause all the attention it deserves. It's amazing what people can do when they put their mind to it and they believe it's what they were chosen for....

Brian Allman

# ABOUT THE AUTHOR

Al DeCesaris on the beach in Ocean City, MD (photo courtesy of Grant L. Gurksy).

Al DeCesaris is an advocate for his niece Jenna and all those suffering with Sturge-Weber Syndrome and is dedicated to creating awareness and raising funds to further the efforts to find a cure. Al is also a public speaker with a focus on motivating people to achieve their goals both personally and professionally, and inspiring them to help those in need.

Al is an attorney as well as the Vice President of *Celebrate Hope Foundation, Inc.*, a nonprofit charitable organization dedicated to improving the quality of life of those affected by Sturge-Weber Syndrome.

Since 2006, he has helped raise over $1,000,000 for the research and treatment of Sturge-Weber Syndrome. These funds have directly supported the work of the Hunter Nelson Sturge-Weber Center at Kennedy Krieger Institute and helped fund research that led to the discovery of the cause of Sturge-Weber Syndrome.

To further the efforts to find a cure, Al DeCesaris is dedicating all profits from the sale of his "For A Cure" books to Sturge-Weber Syndrome research.

To learn more about Al's efforts, please visit www.AlDeCesaris.com

Made in the USA
Middletown, DE
21 September 2016